Death by BS

Navigating through your Blind
Spots to become a Better Leader

HEALY QUINN
PUBLISHERS

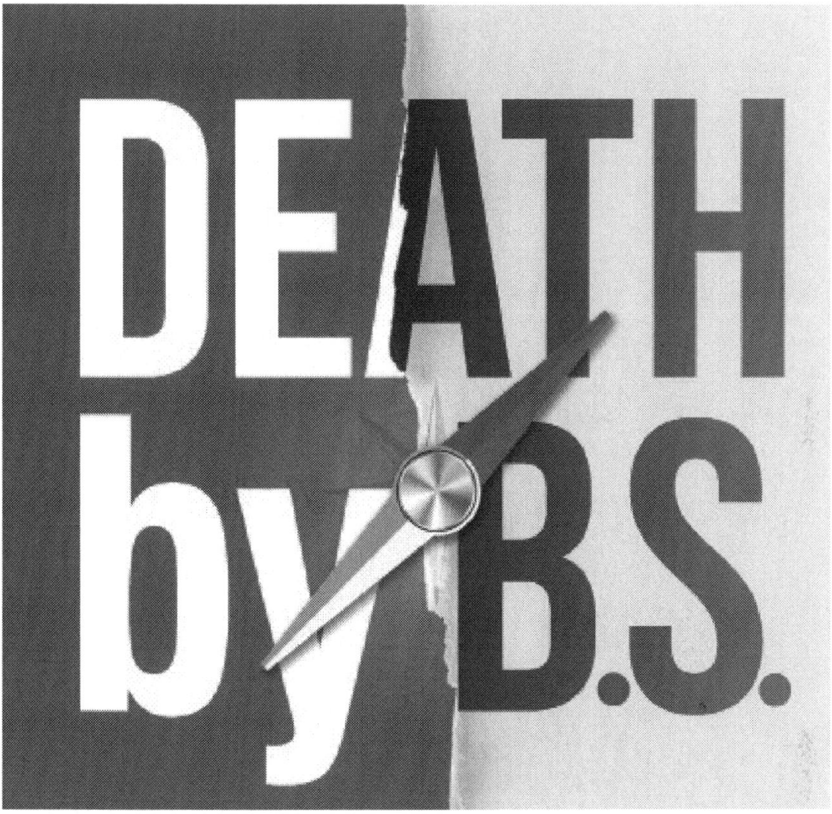
DEATH
by B.S.

Dedication

Bob Burg and Kathy Tagenel for opening my eyes to what it means to not only give, but also to receive.

My Kids, Imaara and Khalid for their strength, support, and encouragement while I was learning to be a dad.

To my Wife, Sam for the unconditional love, support, push, and always having my back.

To my Mom, Brothers Nasir and Amin for raising, supporting and showing me what giving wholeheartedly is about.

They have all played a BIG part in this book.

Last, and most certainly not least, Shannon Peel for her ongoing commitment to help me get the brand out. Imaara for taking the stories I had and making them into my voice, it was a pleasure connecting with her at this level. My Brother from another mother, CJ for his endless love, support, encouragement, and his knack for taking my words and making a story out of them.

Lots of Love to all

Harley Quinn Publishing
17243 Coral Beach Road,
Lake Country,
V4V 1C1

ISBN: 978-1-7776322-0-5
© Copyright 2021 Likky Lavji

HEALY QUINN
PUBLISHERS

Table of Contents

DEATH by B.S.

Introduction

This book is for those who repeatedly come up against the same issue over and over, which impedes their ability to succeed. It will come as no surprise that the way you behave around others has a direct impact on how people react to you. What may come as a surprise is that others see you differently than you see yourself based on how you interact with them.

You may think you are a "happy" person, but your neighbour describes you as grumpy. You might believe you are generous to a fault, but your wife tells her best friend that you are stingy with your resources, gifts, love, or a number of other things in your relationship. You describe yourself as easy going and your co-workers consider you demanding and exacting.

This disconnect between how you perceive yourself and the reality of how others see you is called the blind spot effect. Because of blind spots in your life, you do not realize you are doing certain things and behaving in particular ways.

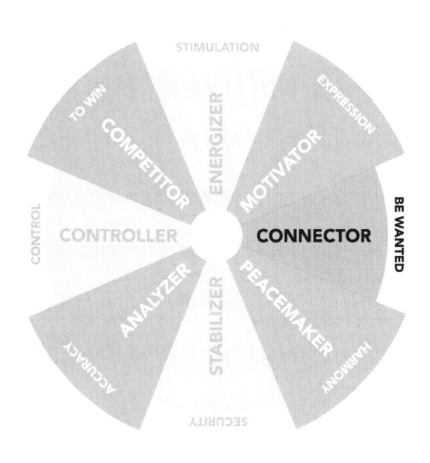

"You Are Not Alone"

Before becoming the Blind Spot Navigator, I owned a small IT company called Matrix. Over ten years I built a profitable business where I was a one-man show doing everything to take care of a strong client base. After ten years of growth, the company was maxed out in billable hours because I only had so much bandwidth. In an effort to take the business to the next level, I decided to bring on people smarter than me to help the business grow.

During my journey to take it to the next level, I came up against the same limitations over and over again. The results were frustrating, the problems were time consuming, and the overhead was expensive. I couldn't see why my efforts to grow kept failing to produce the desired results. I was unaware of how my behaviour was affecting others. My behaviours, beliefs and attitudes were causing my partners and employees to become unmotivated and leave the company. My business became a revolving door, and I could not understand why.

In this book, I will share my journey at Matrix; where I failed, where I succeeded and what I learned about myself. In the process, you will discover blind spots and how they get in the way of your success. You will also learn how to overcome your own blind spots in your day-to-day life.

Pyramid of Results

The purpose of writing this book is to help you achieve success by focusing on results-based actions. Leaders who are results- oriented have a clear understanding of what they want, but their blind spots can get in the way of achieving that result. By interconnecting blind spot identification with results-based leadership, teams are better able to achieve their common objectives and move the whole organization forward.

At the core of this book is the foundation for any team who wants to achieve results – Trust. Through identifying the blind spots around trust, conflict, integrity and accountability, you will be able to lead a team to the results you want through the use of trust. When teams trust each other they are open to voicing ideas, supporting each other, collaborating, and working towards common objectives. Trust is the key to productive teams.

More than a Book

Death by B.S, is more than a book to read, it will challenge you to think about your own blind spots and how you can move beyond them to find the success that eludes you. It is filled with questions to help you identify your blind spots and find the solutions you will need to change and realign your life to gain the success you desire.

The Blind Spot Assessment

On my website, LikkyLavji.com there is a free assessment to help you identify which blind spots may be lurking outside of your peripheral vision. You will be provided with a report identifying your strengths, your work style, and the behaviors that others see, but you may not presently see in yourself. I encourage you to take a moment to take the assessment and read the report unique to your work style.

"We all need to take some time to learn about ourselves and how we show up to the world. Ever been disappointed by someone who promised one thing and delivered another?

I don't think people intentionally deceive their managers, team members, or customers.

This happens because they don't understand the consequential effects of accountability to themselves and others. They believe they can be on time for meetings, when they have a hard time with knowing what time it is, even with a phone in their hand.

We all have blind spots. These are the behaviors that we think we don't have because we want to be seen as, or even believe that we already are, the best versions of ourselves.

When we are honest with ourselves and take a good look at who we are, what we are capable of, and our shortcomings, we can show up every day with integrity and be held accountable because we are living up to our promises.

Take time either weekly, or daily, to look within yourself and get to know the real you."

Matrix
Lacking Trust

Matrix

When I started Matrix IT in 1990, it was all about the trusting relationships I had built with my customers. They trusted me and I trusted them. For ten years I grew the business until it could not grow anymore because of time constraints. As a one-man show based on billable hours, I could only grow so much before I ran out of capacity. In 2010 I made the decision to take my business to the next level by bringing in business partners. As with any business any profits made gets distributed amongst partners. This meant a smaller piece of a pie for me than what I was used to. I was sharing profits however the business wasn't billing out the hours needed to compensate for that sharing. This triggered my scarcity blind spot behaviours and I started making unreasonable demands, pushing them to work harder than they were willing to, and standing over them to make sure they were doing what they said they were. Of course, I ended up creating a toxic environment where failure was the only option for any partnership I entered into.

I'd choose partners who were smarter than me, or at least, whom I thought were smarter. I expected them to have all the answers and when they didn't, I started questioning their skills. I am a 'go getter' and am driven to succeed, so when my partners were not working as hard as I was, I questioned their commitment to the company and started demanding they prove their worth. As doubts about them crept into my mind, my behaviour became more demanding, leading to conflict in the office.

I expected perfection from them. I knew I wasn't perfect, but if I was going to share the profits of my company, they needed to be perfect. They weren't perfect, no one is, and to expect someone to be is unrealistic. The kicker was, they had no idea that I expected them to be perfect.

I'd neglected to communicate my expectation to make the partnership successful because I was scared the conversation would lead to conflict; another of my own blind spot behaviours. Of course, by avoiding conflict, I ended up building resentments that in turn caused conflict, which ultimately led to the dissolution of the partnership.

After the partnership experiment failed, I decided to hire people as employees. Unfortunately, my scarcity blind spot led to behaviours that would ultimately sabotage my relationships with my employees and clients. Due to my scarcity mindset, I micro-managed them and paid them a base wage rather than a premium according to their skillset. I behaved just as I had with my former partners.

I didn't trust them to do the work. I was scared there wasn't enough money for me after I paid them and feared they were going to take my business away from me. These fears were sewn deep inside me from my early childhood years. It wasn't until much later in my life when I recognized that the sudden death of my father when I was 3 years old was the catalyst for a number of my blind spot behaviors.

He was a successful global businessman who provided our family with financial security and an expensive lifestyle. After his death, our financial future was negatively changed, while my extended family's wealth continued to grow, leaving us behind. From the age of 12, I've been trying to find the financial security we'd lost when my dad died, both for myself and my family. So, when the profit pie needed to be shared with partners and employees, my fear of financial reversal flared up from my childhood.

Since I was unaware about what was happening subconsciously, I pushed others, questioned their motives, and micro-managed them in order to force the growth of my IT business. I didn't trust any of my employees to work hard enough, to do the job, or care enough about our clients and my company's bottom line to ensure financial success for my family. To no one's surprise, this caused friction within the office.

When I look back on that time and analyze the reality of the situation without emotion, I discover I had a profitable business which provided a good income for my family and those who worked for me. I should have been happy, content, and proud, but I was scared. I was anxious and grasping at straws, that everything would be taken away, and that my family would end up in the same conditions I experienced as a child.

I acted from a place of fear, saying things I didn't mean and then forgot that I said them because I had passed those feelings to someone else. See, when we live in fear, we look to others to help us without thinking about how we can help them. Our fears spill out of us and we treat others like commodities, tools, and even saviours.

When fear enters our thinking, we say no to opportunities, we refuse to take risks, and we make negative assumptions about others. You know what they say about assumptions, and I was definitely an ass to more than one person who helped build my business. Sometimes it takes a life altering event to shine a light on our shortcomings. This forces us to look hard at who we really are and what we truly want out of life.

That event for me was my wife's breast cancer diagnosis. Suddenly, I was back to where I was when I was 3 years old, faced with the fear of mortality of a loved one. I wanted to be there for Sam as she battled her illness, so I made the decision to step away from my business by hiring a manager to take care of things while I focused on my wife and her health.

For over a year, I did not pay attention to the business and I assumed it would be in shambles when I got back. I did not expect the business to thrive without me. In fact, I expected the mice to play while the cat's away and for the business to be turned upside down. Imagine my surprise when my accountant called and asked me what had happened over the last year. I said, "Well, I was with Sam this year, so I couldn't work, but I'll bring revenues back up when I get back."

He said, "What? No. Your profits are up, significantly."

I was shocked.

The person I'd put in place to manage the business while I was with Sam had grown the business. You'd think I would have made that person a partner, but no, scarcity and fear were front and center in our home the year Sam was beating cancer. I did not value the individual enough or provide him with any appreciation for what he'd done, so he left and started his own firm. Scarcity blinded me to the truth of what I needed to do to keep exceptional talent at the helm.

When I look back at all the people I'd hired and partnered with, I regret my behaviour because, in hindsight, I can see their value and all the good we could have done for the community as a group. We could have shifted the IT world because the intention was there, they had the skills, the values, and the motivation. The missing element was confident leadership, my ability to trust that my team had the skill set and will to get the job done. My blind spots were in the way of leading a team to building a successful and sustainable business.

A scarcity mindset causes us to be blind to the truth of the situation. When I look at my financial health, on paper I am doing very well. I have enough to live a long life and have a good life. While I can see it in black and white, I didn't feel it, so in the back of my mind I always thought, "What if it's not enough?" That fear drove me to go after more, to push for more, and to behave towards others in a manner that caused stress and conflict. However, I couldn't see the problem because it was in my blind spot. It took my brother to help me see myself so I could change.

My brother is a successful automotive professional and we have a close supportive relationship. One day, I was buying a car at his dealership when the salesperson asked me, "Have you noticed a change in your brother?" I told him that I had seen a positive change in his behaviour and interactions with the people around him, but I had no idea why. He looked at me and said, "Yeah, he made us all go to a self and professional development course and it really made a big difference." I was curious, so I went upstairs and asked my brother about the course and then found a class for Sam and me to attend later that week.

It was during one of these classes where I discovered my blind spots and began to understand that I needed to make a change in my life. One of the exercises in the class was for the other students to tell you their impressions of the person in the 'Hot seat', who was not allowed to say anything during this time.

When my turn for the Hot seat came, I was very nervous about what others would say about me. I really didn't want to know. Not knowing was safer than hearing the awful truth. I didn't want to hear how I wasn't welcome, wasn't wanted, wasn't a part of the group. I was sick to my stomach, but I'd made the commitment to take the class, so I sat in the seat to hear what my classmates thought about me.

What they said changed my life. I'd expected to hear negative comments, and some of them were because when I came into the class, I was in full defensive behaviour mode. I was aggressive, cold, and unfriendly. Then as I got to know the people, participated in the conversation, and began to open up I behaved differently. So, there I was, expecting to hear the same messages I heard as a child, when they started to tell me that I was friendly, trusting, caring, a great listener, compassionate, present, a true Go-Giver. By the end I was in tears. How could strangers see these things in me when I did not see them in myself? Didn't they know that I was not supposed to amount to anything? Couldn't they see I was a scared little boy who had everything taken away from him when his dad died? How could I be what they said I was?

This was not the only epiphany that I had while in the course with Sam. When our daughter was born, she was our little princess. She brought us joy, luck and happiness, but boy, was she feisty. So feisty in fact, that her daycare teacher told us "She's so sweet, but she sure does have her head on strong." This was when she was only four months old! By the time she was three she was not only spunky, but she loved to explore. Being headstrong when you can't move is one thing, but when you can run it's quite another!

One summer vacation on our way to Tofino, we stopped for lunch with our friends at a local sandwich stop. After lunch we were all standing around and chatting when our princess decided to head to our vehicle on the other side of the parking lot, passing right in front of an oncoming car! As the car screeched to a halt, only inches away from my daughter, I ran out of the restaurant and into the parking lot to grab her and hold her tight. I then said the words that would shape our relationship for years to come, "I'm never letting you go again."

I'm never letting you go again.

For years, every time my daughter wanted to do something, I'd be there as a shelter hovering over her and making sure she was safe. It ended up creating an awkwardness and distance between us.

She'd say, "Dad you're annoying, paranoid, and over-protective." And well, I was.

I'm never letting you go again.

Teaching

I unconsciously tied the moment of when my daughter was nearly hit by that car to when my dad passed away and I was only three years old. This left me feeling alone, unloved, unsafe and untrusting.

No wonder I wanted to protect her from potential harm, like a helicopter parent hovering overhead. My family would tell me I was being too controlling and overprotective. In my mind, I thought I was just being normal, that there was nothing actually wrong with me. I refused to listen. In reality, however, I was that overprotective and overbearing dad and husband.

I'm never letting you go again.

Fast forward 13 years; I realized this wasn't normal, but I didn't know what to do. I just knew that I had to make a change. Seeking for answers, I attended personal development workshops, went to counsellors, read books, and attended more workshops. Words like "controlling, untrusting, angry, anxious, money, past relationships, narcissist, unhappy" all started to come to light. Yes, this was my BS. My blind spot. It was what I couldn't see but others could. It took me years to acknowledge my BS. I can't imagine the impact this ended up having on my family, employees and friends. The good news is. It doesn't have to take you that long.

As I learned about myself and became more self-aware during the professional development training, I started to behave differently by catching myself and changing how I treated others. I realized that I had to let go of this fear of not having enough and I had to change from a scarcity mindset to one of abundance, or at the very least, a mindset that convinced myself that I did in fact, have enough.

Changing a deeply ingrained, long held belief so you can change your behaviours and be a better version of yourself can be difficult. It takes dedication, courage, and support of like-minded peers who have your best interests at heart. I had to step outside of my comfort zone and ask the people I admired and trusted to help me by giving me their honest feedback and advice. We all fear hearing what others really think about us, our ideas, and our lives, however, without their honest feedback we cannot become better.

I would have never learned these things about myself without the mastermind group I belong to, which is filled with professionals I admire and trust. I believe they have my best interests at heart, and I have theirs. We help each other make decisions, work towards our goals, and call each other out on our BS to ensure we know the truth about who we are and what we are capable of.

My behaviour changed and I was fortunate to bring one of the coaches from the professional development seminars into Matrix to help me grow the business from a place of trust and abundance.

I continued to work on myself and built trust-based relationships with clients and employees to grow Matrix into a firm I could be proud of. In 2014, when I was approached by a US company with an offer to purchase Matrix IT, I was led on a new path of discovery as this coach suggested I also consider coaching because I enjoyed helping other people achieve their goals.

I sold Matrix and became a facilitator for Go-Givers International, a company owned by my good friend and mentor Bob Burg. My goal was to help sales teams build relationships with customers.

As my coaching business grew, I discovered my clients, like me, also had blind spots getting in the way of their success. The more I thought about it the more I realized my purpose was to help them make the necessary changes to achieve the success they wanted for themselves by helping them understand their own blind spots.

Recently, I went out on a bike ride with my wife, Sam. We'd taken a break and I had this huge smile on my face, she looked at me and asked what I was smiling about. I'd just realized I was doing what I loved and was getting paid for it. I was no longer building relationships with the idea of what the other person could do for me, who they could introduce me to, or how much they would pay me. I was instead building trusting relationships based on how I could help people with no expectation of compensation or benefit to myself.

I was building the kind of relationships I had with my Matrix clients when it was just me, no partners, no employees, and no pressure to grow and succeed. At the beginning it was all about how I could help them with their IT issues, to provide them with what they needed to succeed, and provide them with the best experience. Instead of trying to figure out how others can serve me to my advantage, I now focus on helping others by asking what I can give of myself. I feel like I'm myself again.

"While living in time, we can't discern the energetic connection between cause and effect. This is because this energetic connection unfolds in the present. The present, when we aren't conscious of it, becomes a blind spot in our awareness. This blind spot makes it impossible to perceive the energetic connection between all life. We simply don't see the continuity of everything.

To perceive the energetic connection and continuity of all life requires an experiential awareness of the intimate relationship between cause and effect. When we can't recognize this connection, our experience appears chaotic, random, and devoid of purpose. When we live in time, we spend our days seeking the meaning of life. In contrast, when we are present, we enjoy a life saturated with meaning."

- The Presence Process - A Journey Into Present Moment Awareness, Michael Brown

"It all depends on your perception and the perception of those around you. Do you know how others perceive you? Have you asked them to describe your personality, character, or image? You might be surprised - I was...

The intent of our message or behaviour doesn't matter, let's face it, there is a road paved with good intentions leading somewhere not so great...

You could walk into a room thinking you are friendly, approachable, and confident, however the people in the room think you're pompous. That's what I discovered when I asked a group of people what their first impression of me was. It opened my eyes.

You've got a second to make a good impression - are you making the right one or are you being blindsided by your behaviours?"

Biases and
Blind Spots

Biases

"Human beings are poor examiners, subject to superstition, bias, prejudice, and a profound tendency to see what they want to see rather than what is really there."
M. Scott Peck

You think your boss is a jerk and then you and your family run into him at the local coffee shop and, to your surprise, you discover that he is funny, interesting, and thoughtful. You don't understand why your wife keeps saying she's fat when she really isn't. Your best friend is forever boasting and being confrontational with you, saying things you know they don't mean. You get passed over for a promotion and the guy who got it doesn't have the experience or skills you do, but he is well liked by everyone. Life seems to be a popularity contest and you have no clue why you are left out of the running.

What is going on?

We all have blind spots within our lives. The successes and failures of relationships, careers, and our mental and physical well-being are all constantly being affected by our blind spots. They can manipulate our reality and cause us to behave in ways we do not intend to. This can result in others misinterpreting and misunderstanding our intention, which can quickly spiral into conflict or hostility. At times, these misinterpretations or misunderstandings may be due to biases people already possess, and at other times, it is because we do not see how our behaviours affect those around us. The latter is called a Blind Spot.

It's similar to a blind spot when driving. When we make a lane-change without checking our blind spot, we don't see the car beside us, and in response, the other driver honks loudly and obnoxiously because they have interpreted our behaviour as rude and unthoughtful. In reality, however, we simply did not recognize that we had a blind spot and we made a mistake. Blind spots in our lives are just like this. We are unaware of how others perceive us based on our behaviours because our point of view is on the opposite side of interaction. We are focused on the intention whereas the other person is focused on their own interpretation, which is affected by assumptions and biases.

The perceptions of our behaviours determine a lot of things. The friends we have, the promotions we get and the amount of money we make are all aspects of our lives that are affected by the way people perceive us and our actions. This is why understanding our blind spots is important for our long-term success.

Our blind spots are rooted in our own insecurities, our past experiences, and our belief structures. There are a number of different cognitive biases that can explain why we interpret situations in a certain way and why we are blind to the reality of the intentions or truth of others.

Truth is subjectively based on emotions, perceptions, biases, and experiences. Two people can witness the same accident and have two very different stories about it. Two people can have the same traumatic event happen to them, but process and deal with the trauma in two very different ways. When we understand ourselves, we reduce blind spots, come closer to the truth, and our intentions become aligned with our behaviours.

Biases

The root cause of our blind spots stem from something that is called cognitive biases. This type of bias can cause us to behave in certain ways or interpret the behaviours of others inaccurately. A cognitive bias is an error in decision making due to personal beliefs, experiences, and assumptions.

It is natural for us to draw from our experiences and knowledge to help us make split decisions about the world around us. At times, our bias is useful and helps us grow. Most times however, biases can easily flaw the data that we use to help us make decisions. This is especially apparent when we have experienced certain events or results that we do not want to repeat.

A recently divorced person may make assumptions about the person they are on a first date with if they exhibit a similar trait or characteristic as their ex. Many become jaded about the opposite gender when they begin to paint the whole gender with the same brush due to their biased point of view. A parent may be overly indulgent because their parents were either strict or withheld their love to get their children to behave a certain way. A person may be excessively cautious at work and take a long time to complete a task because their last manager was always berating them whenever they made the tiniest of mistakes.

It is of course important to learn from our mistakes, but we also need to balance our own lessons with the truth of what is happening at that moment. Our snap judgments about those around us keep us safe from being hurt again and keep us from developing new relationships or discovering new opportunities.

Over the next few pages you will be introduced to different biases and their definitions. Take some time to think about each one and write real world examples of people displaying these biases or how these biases affect your own decision making processes.

Confirmation Bias

Confirmation bias is the tendency to gravitate to facts which confirm your already-held beliefs. You seek out news and stats to back up your argument. You talk to people who have the same opinions as you and avoid conversations with those who disagree with you. You will dismiss anyone who disagrees with you as a liar, fake news, and outright wrong in order to hold on to your point of view. By finding people who confirm your beliefs, you are able to be right no matter what your argument is.

What examples of confirmation bias in the world can you think of?

Overconfidence or Self-Serving Bias

Overconfidence or self-serving bias is a more personalized extension of the confirmation bias, where you have a false sense of your skills, talents, and abilities. Those who are overconfident will believe they can do something they've never done before and if they succeed it's because of their innate skill, and if they fail, it was bad luck and the fault of others stopping them from doing what they needed to do to succeed.

What examples of overconfidence or self-serving bias in the world can you think of?

The Actor Observer Bias

The Actor Observer Bias is when you excuse your short comings, mistakes, and losses due to situations in your life. You were late to the meeting because you had jet lag and couldn't wake up in time. However, if someone else was to do the exact same thing for the exact same reason you blame it on their inability to be responsible. In other words, excuses for failure only apply to you whereas others are personally flawed, incapable, and irresponsible.

What examples of actor observer bias in the world can you think of?

The False-Consensus Effect

The False-Consensus Effect is when someone overestimates how many people agree with them. For example, they assume everyone in the room agrees with them yet their argument is constantly being questioned in discussions. They do not hear or see the reality around them because they believe they are always right and everyone thinks exactly like they do.

What examples of the false-consensus effect in the world can you think of?

Incentive-Caused Bias

Incentive-caused bias is acting a certain way because the incentives are aligned to get you to make a certain decision or take a directed action. Those with vested interest in a decision outcome will attempt to guide another person in the direction of their own benefit, usually regardless of the welfare of the one being led. It is common to use framing bias (next) to do this.

What example of Incentive-caused bias in the world can you think of?

Framing Bias

This bias is on the receiving end of incentive-caused bias. Framing is the means used on you to have you make a decision because of how information is presented to you instead of relying only on the facts. It is a regular tool of the sales professional to create a framing bias to help you make the decision they want you to make. Framing will be used to trigger another's urge to act for the good of their own incentive of gain.

What example of Framing Bias in the world can you think of?

The Optimism Bias

The Optimism Bias is when we tend to be too optimistic for our own good. We overestimate the likelihood that good things will happen to us while underestimating the probability that negative events will impact our lives. The opposite of this is Pessimism Bias.

What example of optimism or pessimism bias in the world can you think of?

The Narrative Fallacy

The Narrative Fallacy occurs because stories help make sense of things and we can relate to them. We are able to tell ourselves a story about a situation to make us look like the hero or the victim. Victimization language revolves around narrative fallacy.

What example of narrative fallacy in the world can you think of?

The Anchoring Bias

Anchoring Bias is when we use pre-existing data as a reference point for all subsequent data and it skews our decision-making processes because we can't see the new data independently of what we've already learned. When A happens then B occurs the first time so we assume every time we do A we get B.

What example of Anchoring Bias in the world can you think of?

The Hindsight Bias

Hindsight Bias is when someone predicts something which turns out wrong and they change their story to, "I knew it all along, I was just kidding before." It is a common cognitive bias of people to see events, even random ones, as more predictable than they are.

The hindsight bias occurs for a combination of reasons, including our ability to "misremember" previous predictions, our tendency to view events as inevitable, and our tendency to believe we could have foreseen certain events. Our memories of events tend to be influenced by what happened after the actual event. This is known as the misinformation effect. A person who witnesses a car accident or crime might believe that their recollection is crystal clear, but researchers have found that memory is surprisingly susceptible to even very subtle influences.

What example of Hindsight bias in the world can you think of?

Loss or Pain Aversion

Emotions can cloud our judgment and lead to poor decisions. The Pain-avoiding psychological denial is the tendency to wish for something to be true to the point we cannot see the actual truth. Someone whose loved one is dying may be in denial and will dismiss the doctor's diagnosis as incompetence or convince themselves the person has a 100% chance of pulling through, when in reality, they only have a 10% chance. Parents of soldiers missing in action may believe their child will be home at any moment, even decades later.

Loss Aversion is the tendency for people to not take risks because they are too scared they will lose what they have or won't succeed so why try.

What example of Loss or Pain Aversion in the world can you think of?

The Representative Bias

Representative Bias happens when people believe there is a correlation between objects, people, and events because they have similar characteristics. A hiring manager may decide not to hire a candidate because they have a beard, like the person they just fired for incompetence. New parents may pass on a name because the kids they know with that name are hyperactive.

What example of Representative Bias in the world can you think of?

The Halo Effect Bias

The Halo Effect Bias or Physical Attractiveness Stereotype is the idea that if something is beautiful, it is good or right. Advertisers, Hollywood, and all media use or buy into this bias. In contrast, in times past, old women with deformities were tried as witches because they looked the part.

What example of the Halo Effect bias in the world can you think of?

The Martyr Bias

When facilitating a strategy session with a client, I like to check in to see where people are at. The following outlines an actual scenario that happened:

The first person expresses excitement about the session. The second begins with a complaint, "It's going to be a tough couple of days, I have all these projects to manage and not sure I can get them all done." The third responds with almost a whimper, "I'm so tired! The kids kept me awake and I've been up since 4 and I'm already on my 4th cup of coffee." All of this, and the CEO replies, "I'm ok, I was up early as well. In fact, I sent all of you an email at 5 to make sure you received this week's action items."

Good grief!

Pass the tissues already. Martyr bias takes on the feeling of voluntary suffering as some sort of self-fulfilling and required penalty for enduring what needs to be done to live a successful life. Bemoaning this personally inflicted adversity seems to beget internal accolades for living according to what is elevated as almost a sort of religious work-ethic. This brings to mind a comical scene in a movie where the emotional martyr is asked, "But did you DIE!?"

After some conversations around the table, they all realized that since one person started it, the rest simply jumped on the bandwagon. For the next 3 days, we had fun calling out when someone played the martyr.

A few months later in a follow up meeting, the team was energized and working through some really big issues. This was only made possible by dealing with a huge blind spot that was contagious.

Another similar story comes from when I had my IT company. The staff and I were at our Monday morning meeting and I started out in similar fashion by asking why nobody had bothered to respond to my email from 4 am. To this, my senior sales rep shot back with, "I'm sorry you were up at 4 this morning, did you expect us to be as well?" and laughed it off.

This hit me hard. In reflection, I realized I was being a martyr, playing the victim, and probably wanted the attention. While difficult to relay in the current meeting, it had to be said. Dealing with this up front made way for bigger victories later.

What example of Martyr Bias in the world can you think of?

Bias Review

Before you make decisions about others, think about these cognitive biases and how they are causing blind spots in your life. Put a check beside each bias that has gotten in your way of making a decision:

- Confirmation Bias
- Overconfidence Bias
- Actor Observer Bias
- False- Consensus Effect
- Incentive-Caused Bias
- Framing Bias
- Optimism or Pessimism Bias
- Narrative Fallacy
- Anchoring Bias
- Hindsight Bias
- Loss or Pain Aversion
- Representative Bias
- Halo Effect Bias
- Martyr Bias

Review your real-world answers to the various bias examples. Have you ever been blinded by your bias when assessing a situation or person?

"Do you live an authentic life or are you always searching for who you should be?

When we are constantly searching for meaning in our lives we can miss seeing who we truly are and the impact we are having on the world around us.

Are you trying to be what you think others expect you to be?

Perhaps, you feel the need to constantly be more than you believe you are.

I want to challenge you to experience the moment by being in it. To be fully aware and present in the moment. To just be who you are and not the "Who" you think the world wants you to be."

Trust and
a Lack of It

Trust and a Lack of It

"I think the currency of leadership is transparency. You've got to be truthful. I don't think you should be vulnerable every day, but there are moments where you've got to share your soul and conscience with people and show them who you are, and not be afraid of it."
-- *Howard Schultz*

Lack of Trust comes from a heartbreak stemming from family, personal relationships, or abuse and trauma. Lack of trust doesn't occur because of something you've done. It occurs as a result of something being done to you. Our minds are like piggy banks; full of our perceptions and memories, which we tend to hold onto forever. For me, it was my father dying and leaving us alone without his guidance and protection. It was the bullies in school parroting their parent's bigotry and racist attitudes. It was the betrayal of those in positions of power in my life, who took advantage of me for their own selfishness instead of ensuring I was supported. When the actions of others cause us to lose something or their inaction results in us having to get through the hard times alone, our ability to trust others is eroded.

Trust in others is cultivated during our childhood and there are numerous factors that can cause us to grow into distrusting adults who behave in a defensive manner to ensure we don't get hurt again. If parents are inconsistent in their messaging or live by the "Do as I say not as I do" method of parenting, their children may grow up believing most people lie or do the opposite of what they say they will. If a parent has anger issues and constant outbursts of anger for the littlest of things, they may grow up scared to make any mistakes. Parents do the best they can with the resources they have. They do not mean to pass on their blind spot behaviours or negative beliefs about themselves to their children. All parents affect their children in different ways and as adults running on autopilot, we run the risk of behaving in ways we do not mean to and passing those behaviours on to our children.

What is the Meaning of Trust?

The Oxford Dictionary defines trust as, "A firm belief in the reliability, truth, ability, or strength of someone or something". For example, we trust people who are benevolent toward us, who have integrity, and whose actions correspond to their words. We trust someone we can count on to consistently do what is, "Right." In an intimate relationship, we trust our partner if he or she is predictable, reliable, and honest.

Trust can also be defined as a verb: Actions based on having confidence or trust in oneself. On an action level, trust involves being able to, "Do something without fear or misgiving."

In organizations, the tone of trust is set by leaders. When leaders create a consistent and nonthreatening place by allowing for feedback and appreciation, they create a trust building relationship because people feel safe. To sum up, organizational trust drives employee engagement and organizational results.

A lot of people don't trust that other people can do the job properly or they don't trust other people to give them the responsibility and tools to lead a team. Lack of Trust comes from our experiences in life with other people. It is the heartbreak, harsh words, betrayals, and disappointments we experience that form how we trust.

I had a hard time trusting those I loved would be with me throughout my life and it affected my behaviours towards everyone around me. When my daughter was three, she was almost hit by a car and at that moment, I said the words, "I'm never letting you go." Over time that promise turned into the words, "I don't trust you." I said the words, "I'm never letting you go," for 12 years and as a result, I became a helicopter parent, too scared to let her do anything without me protecting her from a negative outcome. I thought I was building a trusting relationship because she'd know I was there to protect her. However, her interpretation of my behaviour was, "Dad doesn't trust me," which affected our relationship negatively. My behaviours were having the opposite effect of what I'd intended.

I behaved like that with everyone; my family, my teams at work, my employees, my friends, and everyone around me. By treating everyone like they needed me to hover over them, improve them, and solve their problems, I wasn't trusting them to show up, to do their jobs, or be safe. I was negatively impacting my relationships and causing unnecessary conflict.

Trust is an issue when people don't communicate and don't get to really know each other. Today, it's all about texting, communicating over email, and a quick casual, "Hello."

Think about the friendships you have. Do you trust the people whom you know really well? To trust your teams, family, and friends, you have to get to know them. To build high quality, trusting relationships, you have to connect with them on a personal level. Take the time to get to know more about their family, what they do for fun, what they struggle with, and what they want out of life.

Trust and Leadership

Without trust, workplace culture is hard to achieve, results don't happen, communication doesn't happen. If you are a leader of a team, you have to build trust and to do that, you have to be vulnerable enough to be honest with the people on the team. Open communication is clear, concise, and enables others to understand your intent. For example, you can say, "You know, the last project we worked on, I had a real challenge getting the data for the reports in time to meet my deadline. How can you help me to ensure our reports are accurate and on time?" When you allow the space to open up, others can step up, contribute, and grow trust in you. Once you do that, things change, the culture starts changing, and accountability happens.

You must behave and act according to the level of trust each person has with you. There are different levels of trust and it is important to be appropriate with how much you share based on the level of trust you have with each person. You shouldn't tell the stranger sitting next to you on the bus your deepest, darkest, most shameful secrets. However, you can talk about the weather, the neighbourhood, and a movie you just saw. When talking with an old friend you can talk about personal issues in your marriage, with your kids, and share stories about your family. With co-workers you can talk about the project you're working on, what you did on the weekend, and where you are going on vacation. Being appropriate in your conversations will lead to deeper, vulnerable conversations where you can build trust.

I have a small group that I trust as my inner circle of influence and support. I have boundaries and I set those boundaries really tight by using something I call the "Red Velvet Rope Method." If you're on one side of the velvet rope, you are in my inner circle of trust and I trust you one hundred percent. If you're on the other side of the rope, I trust you, however, I am always verifying to grow my trust in you. If my trust in you isn't growing, you stay on the other side of the velvet rope as a casual acquaintance. If you grow in my trust, at some point, you will be invited past the velvet rope into my inner trusted circle. It is important to understand the different levels of trust you should have with each person in your life and act accordingly so other people will be comfortable with you and trust you enough to open up to the next level of trust.

Trusting others when we've been hurt is difficult. Being vulnerable is scary. Knowing how much to trust someone and how much information to communicate is a skill you will develop with practice. Start small. Tell your team about one thing you need their help with to discover who steps up and then grow your trust with that person. It takes time, evidence, and results to grow trust, however, the first step towards better relationships with people is being vulnerable enough to take the risk to trust in the first place.

There are a number of factors that can cause us to grow into distrusting adults who behave in a defensive manner to ensure we don't get hurt again. The lack of trust blind spot is full of knee jerk behaviours we engage in to keep ourselves 'safe' from others. The parent who tells their teen daughter, "Boys won't love you if you aren't a virgin." out of fear of teen pregnancy or hurtful gossip. The single guy who ghosts a woman by not messaging her after connecting with a woman who reminds him of his ex-girlfriend who cheated on him. The hiring manager who passes on a great candidate because they fear they will outshine them and will have to compete against them for their next promotion. Whatever the reason, when we are not aware of our own lack of trust, we behave in ways which will hurt the ones we love, keep us from fulfilling relationships and limiting the opportunities for our professional success.

Journalling Prompt:

Think back to the events in your life and make a list of all the times someone caused you pain, loss, and isolation.

Take a moment to think about how your behaviours protected you from being victimized again. What did others do to cause you to feel defensive and how did you react when you felt threatened?

These blind spot behaviours are painting a different version of who you are to the world around you. How would you rather react when you feel threatened?

Building a Trusting Team

Your blind spots affect every aspect of your life; how you show up in relationships and how you react to others is just a part of it. Every single one of your actions causes either a positive or negative impact on others, who then react either positively or negatively towards you. This cycle can cause an issue to escalate out of control or an emotionally charged situation to explode. In a professional environment these reactions can impact a person's future opportunities for advancement and the team's effectiveness to succeed.

Lack of trust can creep into business life without you knowing it. Personally, I had a real hard time trusting my teams could do the job right at work. I wasn't open to listening to feedback from employees because I had built a fortress around me to make sure I was safe first. Seemed quite natural for my subconscious mind to be doing this after having experienced certain losses in my life. However, by treating everyone like I didn't trust them, I negatively impacted my relationships by causing unnecessary conflict.

As a leader, you will need the tools to understand the situation and how to defuse any negative emotional build up.

What does a lack of trust in an organization look like?

Leaders who don't trust their teams will create toxic environments by breeding distrust in each other, inside and outside of the team. Here are some of the behaviours a lack of trust creates in people.

In Sales:

If I am a salesperson and the potential customer tells me he doesn't know what he wants, I may become defensive because I think he's playing a game to pull the wool over my eyes. In this case, I might become pushy and challenge his statement to make him feel dumb, so he'll tell me what I want to know. I may stop listening to the person and start telling him what I think he wants, after all, I'm the one who knows all about the product or service and how it helps people. I will take control of the interaction to force the potential customer to agree with me and buy my product or service.

In Leadership:

If I am a team leader and I don't trust my team, I won't give them important tasks to complete. I'll do all the work myself and become overloaded while my team struggles with purpose and direction. I may even start complaining to other leaders that my team members are useless and ineffective, impacting their futures with the company, along with my own. If I do assign tasks, I'll hover over team members to ask them questions about where they are in the process and how they are doing with the task. I will micromanage to the point where my team members feel uninspired, powerless, and unmotivated. Nothing gets done and the whole team misses deadlines or targets, and it affects our opportunities within the organization.

In Service:

A lack of trust in customer service manifests as blame instead of help. When a customer calls with a complaint about a product the customer service advisor will immediately blame the customer for not using it properly or doing something to break the item. The fault is not with the company or the employee; it is instead the customer's fault. Teams will see this behaviour whenever a problem comes up or a project does not go smoothly. Instead of finding solutions, a team steeped in distrust will cover their butts by shifting blame to some-one else. No one takes responsibility for the problem and it is up to everyone else to fix it.

What Trusting Behaviour Looks Like

When we trust people, it shows, and everyone wins because the environment is one of collaboration, productivity, and support. Leaders who lead with trust in their people are supportive, transparent, and helpful. Opportunity flows to trust based teams.

In Sales:

When we trust people, we are open to them and their needs. We create an environment where they feel safe to share their needs and wants with us. Trust based sales focus on the relationship with the person, not the transaction of the product or service, to provide clients with solutions that meet their needs. If I trust a person, I'm doing business with I take what they say at face value and negotiate with them to come up with a win-win solution. I am more concerned with their happiness than I am with my commission to ensure they will want to return or send their friends to me because they trust me to take care of them. Trust based sales is not a short-term gain approach, it is a long-term success method. It may seem like the only hard road initially but paves the highway for future collaboration and success. It can be difficult now, or difficult later; this is a choice.

In Leadership:

Trust based leadership provides a safe place for employees to contribute, work, and grow. If I'm a trust-based leader, I will delegate work to others based on their skill sets and abilities to get the job done and I will trust them to meet the clearly set out directions and deadlines I have provided. I will check in with them to see where we are as a team on the project to ensure everyone is getting the help they need to stay on target. I will provide my team with the opportunity to prove themselves and grow their skill sets by helping them, instead of giving them tasks I know they are capable of doing and learning from. When there is conflict within the team, I will mediate to help them solve their problems on their own. As a trust-based leader, I lead through example, teaching, and support.

In Service:

Client service teams who interact with customers from a place of trust will help solve their problem and provide service which grows the client's trust in the company and brand. When a customer calls with a complaint about a product the customer service rep will listen, understand, and provide a safe place for the customer to vent their frustration. They will take ownership of the problem and find a solution which will satisfy the client while keeping the company's integrity intact. They don't give away the farm to make someone happy, they provide the right solution for the problem at hand while ensuring the customer feels they are taken care of. This is a delicate balance.

Trust and Vulnerability

Members of great teams trust one another on a fundamental, and emotional level. They are comfortable being vulnerable with each other about their weaknesses, mistakes, fears, and behaviors. They get to a point where they can be completely open with one another, without filters. Trust is all about vulnerability and team members who trust one another are open about their failures, weaknesses, and fears. Vulnerability-based trust is seen in people who can admit the truth about themselves and do not engage in time wasting unprofessional behaviour. This type of trust is rare because life experiences reduce our ability to put ourselves at risk for the good of others. Protecting ourselves is understandable, however, this can also be the one behaviour that can be lethal for a team and its productivity. It's important we say things like "I was wrong," "I made a mistake," "I need help," "I'm not sure," "You're better at this than I am," and even, "I'm sorry." If we are honest and upfront, we deal with issues instead of worrying about what everyone else thinks or their agendas.

For example, if a CFO always questions items on expense reports, colleagues may believe her motivation is one of control or lack of trust. However, if colleagues understand she grew up in a poor family, with financially conservative parents who demanded she account for every penny spent, or she was blamed for missing co-workers past fraud, they may be more understanding. They can still question the CFO and request more funds, but they won't call the CFOs character into question. They will be able to focus on a solution to the problem without hurt feelings and mudslinging.

Trust lies at the heart of a functioning and cohesive team, without it, teamwork cannot occur. Trust comes from the vulnerability of team members' sharing their weaknesses, skill deficiencies, interpersonal shortcomings, mistakes, requests for help, and so on. This type of trust enables us to focus on the job at hand rather than on protecting ourselves, our turf, or our individual jobs. Building trust takes time, trusted leadership, and a safe environment to be vulnerable.

Ask Yourself in Hindsight

Deep Dive

In this part of the book you are given lots of space to write, doodle, and draw to understand your level of trust and those who trust you. This isn't a test. I will never see your answers. Neither will anyone else if you don't want them to. This exercise and all the other exercises in this book are meant only for you. This is your truth. If you want to discover your truth, then you must be 100% honest with yourself.

The questions are meant to get your mind thinking about behaviour, blind spots, and trust from different points of view. Whether you write the words, doodle images, or draw pictures to get your truth out on paper is up to you. Perhaps you want to record your answers using an app on your phone or computer and then play the answers back to yourself. There are a number of ways for you to answer these questions, use the method which works best for you.

Checklist A

- [ ] Avoid conflict
- [ ] Communication is vague and spinning of the truth
- [ ] Don't value the contributions of team members
- [ ] Blame others, circumstances, and processes for failures
- [ ] Control of information, tasks, and won't share with others
- [ ] Fail to keep your promises, agreements and commitments
- [ ] Micromanage and resist delegating.
- [ ] Inconsistency between what you say and how you behave
- [ ] Scapegoating others
- [ ] Judge blame and criticize rather than offer feedback
- [ ] Do not allow others to contribute or make decisions
- [ ] Refuse to compromise to foster win-lose arguments
- [ ] Refuse to be held accountable by your colleagues.
- [ ] Don't discuss your personal life
- [ ] Aren't vulnerable
- [ ] Don't ask colleagues for help
- [ ] Take suggestions and critiques as personal attacks
- [ ] Refuse to follow through on decisions
- [ ] Secret back-door negotiations to create alliances
- [ ] Refuse to apologize

Checklist B

- [ ] Are Transparent with intentions
- [ ] Say what they mean and mean what they say
- [ ] Asks for team member input & feedback
- [ ] Understands failures are part of the process not a fault
- [ ] Is a resource of information for others to go to
- [ ] Can count on them to get the job done
- [ ] Enables teammates to do their job
- [ ] What you see is what you get
- [ ] Takes responsibility for actions
- [ ] Gives constructive feedback
- [ ] Supports teammates
- [ ] Negotiates to ensure win-win
- [ ] Mediates conflict
- [ ] Shares appropriate personal stories
- [ ] Are vulnerable
- [ ] Asks for help
- [ ] Focused on solutions not problems
- [ ] Apologizes for mistakes
- [ ] Acts for the good of the team
- [ ] People trust them

Which checklist has more checkmarks? A or B?

If checklist A, you need help, your team is highly distrusting of each other and are not working together to meet your organization's objectives.

If checklist B, you have a team of trusting people who are working together to move towards your team's objectives.

If checklist A & B are approx. equal, you have a team of mixed levels of trust, which is impeding your team's overall success. You will need to work with your team to build trust between members.

Go back and make a list of those behaviours from Checklist A, which you will need to be aware of and find solutions to move team members from distrustful to trustful supportive team members.

Ask yourself

Following are a number of questions with space for you to place your answers to help you redefine your team and yourself to be more trusting and supportive of each other.

What is the most disruptive lack of trust behaviour affecting your team?

When you think of trust in a team, what words come to mind?

What are the best trust behaviours or your team?

Do you often find yourself needing to be in control of your team?

List your fears, worries, and doubts:

Go back over your list of fears, worries, and doubts.
Put a sad face beside those which are a result of a lack of trust.
Put an upside down face beside those which are irrational.
Put a checkmark beside those you can take action on to fix.

Do you generally feel your team can't be trusted?

Why is trust easy or difficult for you? Where does your trust issues
come from? What is at their root?

Whom do you Trust? List everyone you trust.

Put a:

Checkmark next to those who know your embarrassing moments.
Star beside everyone who knows your darkest secrets.

Dollar signs beside those you can ask for money without shame.

Smiley face beside those you can call to bail you out of jail.

Heart beside those who will not shame you, belittle you, judge you,
kick you when you're down, no matter what you've done.

Write about a time you were having a really bad day, a huge problem, something emotionally charged, embarrassing, hard to voice.

Who did you call for help?

Why did you call them?

What did they do when you asked for help?

How did they respond to what you had to say?

Why did you feel safe talking to them?

What did they say to you?

Did they say anything to cause you emotional pain or shame?

What was their body language? Did they lean in or sit back?

Were their arms open or crossed?

Did you feel they were present and listening?

How do you know they were listening?

Did they talk about your problem or about them?

What is it about this person that makes you feel you can go to them with anything?

Do people trust you?

Write about the last time leadership came to you to solve a problem the company was having.

Write about the last time a colleague came to you with a serious problem that may affect their success within the company.

Write about a time one of the team members you lead brought a problem to you.

Write about the last time a friend came to you for help, talked to you about a serious problem, or was vulnerable with you.

Write about the last time your spouse / partner / lover came to you to ask for help

What did you do?

Did you listen?

Did you give unsolicited advice trying to solve the problem?

Did you make a joke?

Did you berate them in any way?

Say something inappropriate?

Judge them as less because of it?

Shut your eyes. Take a moment to picture the conversation.

How did they approach you?

Were they open, hesitant, shameful, or insecure?

What did you say?

Did you lean back in your chair and cross your arms or did you lean in to listen?

Were you busy figuring out what advice to give?

Thinking about some task you needed to do?

Or Were you present and listening?

Did you change the topic?

Deflect any blame? Feel defensive?

How did you feel at the time?

Matrix
in Conflict

Matrix

At Matrix I avoided the vulnerable conversations because I didn't want to face anything hinting. I'd made a mistake or that I didn't know what I was doing. It was easier for me to push, make demands, and micro-manage rather than voice my expectations and listen to my staff's opinions. I avoided conflict altogether, resulting in avoiding healthy conflict, which would have in turn opened possibilities, sparked innovative ideas, and provided clarity of expectation.

My fear of conflict blind spot resulted in self protectionist behaviour throughout my life. I was scared that if I confronted staff on certain things or told them what I really wanted from them, they would leave Matrix and possibly take my clients with them.

When you fear conflict, you don't communicate clearly, or you hold back important information needed to provide the results you want. I was constantly disappointed and frustrated because targets weren't being met. Either that, or they would meet the wrong target of closing a certain number of tickets instead of solving the client's IT problems.

To avoid conflict, I was focused on the data metrics instead of the relationships with my staff and this caused an undercurrent of silent conflict in the office.

When I was made aware of my behaviours and how they were affecting my staff, I dug deep into myself to try to discover why I feared having open and honest communication with my staff.

Why did I fear having those tough conversations about expectations, performance, and results?

As with most blind spots, the answer was found in my childhood. We moved to Canada from Uganda and Pakistan when I was 10 and enrolled in a new school where the kids made fun of me for being different. Some even told me to go back to where I came from. I felt unwelcome and was attacked on a regular basis.

This experience lurked in my mind as a blind spot and ended up impacting how I treated others in order to keep them from hurting me. I would do my best to not rock the boat by talking about anything emotionally charged or to give them the opportunity to say something negative about me.

Since I was bullied as a kid, I developed a stutter, making it harder for me to communicate clearly with others. Whenever I felt uncomfortable, vulnerable, and insecure, my stutter would get worse, and I'd shut down in order to protect myself from being judged or ridiculed. Avoiding bullies and conflict became a natural behaviour.

Uncovering my feelings about being bullied led me to face the pressures my family placed on me growing up. I had a lot to live up to because my family told me, "You're just like your dad: passionate, caring, and driven."

Being compared to a father who died when he was still a perfect superman in the eyes of his sons, and not yet the flawed man we would have gotten to know as adults, created an ideal which was impossible to live up to. This comparison stayed with me and pushed me hard to live up to their expectations and make my dad proud.

My family valued success and pushed us to be the best versions of ourselves and create wealth for our family. My paternal grandfather was strict, loving, family focused, and a very powerful man in the community. He was wealthy and instilled the values of education, hard work, and wealth into each generation. It was important to build wealth and security for the family and you did this by doing your best.

On my mother's side, they worked hard and were frugal with their money because though they were not wealthy, they were careful with what they had. In my family if you didn't behave in the expected manner, you found yourself in conflict with multiple adults.

I was an angry immature teenager who didn't have a strong authoritative hand at home to keep me in line. I was raised by a single mom doing her best with the support available to her. I was lost and this caused her to worry. I remember one day when I was skipping school, yet again, I answered a knock at the door and this big muscular man was in my face telling me to get my act together. He was a family friend I'd looked up to and here he was, in my face with an angry disapproving tone, telling me I was a screw up.

This opinion was backed up by two of my aunts who told me, "Likky, you are a difficult boy, you won't amount to anything in life." Just imagine how destructive this can be for a moment. Their words stuck with me, limiting my belief system. This was a seed from which my blind spots grew. At the time, they were scared and worried for me and acted in the way they'd been shown by my grandfathers. They said what they did, not because they truly believed I was of no value, but in hoping to get me to, 'tow the line' and get back on track. My teenage brain interpreted it as evidence that I was not good enough to have good things in life. Perception is vital, but in our formative years, such events can be destructive.

Throughout my life, I have been trying to prove them wrong by pushing to acquire more and be successful. I did build a successful IT business. I have money to do the things I enjoy doing, go on vacations, and buy things I want. I own a gorgeous home in a highly sought-after community and am able to pay for things my children need to have a successful future, like an education. Yet, I was not happy. I could not find joy in my life because it wasn't ever enough to overcome my aunts' prediction for my life. I constantly compared my life to my uncles, aunts, and cousins. In my mind, I did not have enough to be considered successful. Despite a prosperous exterior, this self-fulfilling prophecy was bearing fruit in the garden of my consciousness. No matter what I had in my hand, it didn't satisfy the lack in my mind.

I didn't approach them to ask what they thought of me now as an adult. I didn't voice my frustrations about the things they had said to me, done, or taken from my future because my mom wanted to keep relationships with my dad's family cordial. We had to stay silent about any grievances, hurts, and transgressions of their words and behaviours. Any anger we may have harboured against my dad's brothers was to be put aside for the greater good of a peaceful family. Fighting for what was in our best interests was not allowed, we were to remain silent, listen to what they said, and be good children.

Throughout my life, the message of conflict avoidance was drilled into me, however, by avoiding the negative conflict it became ingrained that I had to avoid all conflict. This affected my success at Matrix because instead of clearly communicating expectations and having healthy debates to come up with a compromise, I engaged in passive aggressive behaviour to get what I wanted from my staff.

I'd pushed for a high number of tickets to be cleared and with the limited number of hours in a day, this meant they needed to do the work fast. When they rapidly did their work, they didn't fix the real problem and a new ticket would be submitted the next day.

This way, they would only fix the next symptom instead of taking the time to fix the actual problem. They were meeting their targets, but they weren't doing the best job because they didn't have the time to dedicate to each issue to discover the real solution.

You can probably see what the result was -- increased tickets and decreased customer satisfaction. We'd moved from focusing on quality relationships with our clients to a transactional interaction with them and their trust in us began to fade.

The more complaints from clients resulted in more conflict because I'd react without thinking and push my staff without giving them a chance to voice their concerns back to me. When I finally took the time to work on my business, I saw how we'd moved from relationship focus to transaction focus and I wanted to go back to a relationship-based approach. To change the behaviours of my staff meant I first had to face up to my blind spot behaviours.

John Maxwell calls a Blind Spot "an area in the lives of people in which they continually do not see themselves or their situation realistically. This unawareness often causes great damage to the people and those around them."

"Conflict occurs when we think we are always right and those who disagree with us are wrong. Conflict is simply the energy created by the gap between what we want and what we're experiencing," says Nate Regier, a former practicing psychologist and author of Conflict Without Casualties (Berrett-Koehler, 2017). "If we define conflict as energy that's created by the gap, then the real question is 'How are we going to use that energy?'"

Do you avoid conflict, embrace it, or use it to get your way?"

Seeking or
Avoiding Conflict

Conflict

"Conflict is simply the energy created by the gap between what we want and what we're experiencing…If we define conflict as energy that's created by the gap, then the real question is 'How are we going to use that energy?'"

Nate Regier, a former practicing psychologist and author of Conflict Without Casualties (Berrett-Koehler, 2017)

Conflict can cause us to lose trust in someone or it can help us to build trust depending on how we approach it and use it. Conflict has a negative connotation in the English language. However, it has a positive result when managed properly. It can help us to see things from a different point of view, it can lead to innovative ideas, and creative solutions to our problems.

We fear conflict because we do not want to face our shortcomings by being told what is wrong with us, after all we all have our own long list of flaws. We do not want others to judge us, shame us, or hurt us so we avoid conflict. Fear of conflict is based in distrust of the people you are in conflict with.

On the opposite side of the conflict coin are those who have a short fuse and engage in conflict to solve their problems, defend their positions, and ensure they are not being taken advantage of.

These people are angry when slighted and might feel they have no control over their lives, their futures, or their success. They feel under-valued, attacked, and have no trust in anyone. There are those who revel in conflict and love it because it makes them feel powerful to make others feel like less. They love to troll the internet trying to get people fired, ostracized, and proven wrong.

There is also healthy conflict. People who debate ideas to find the best course of action are in conflict and yet, because they are in a 'safe' place with people whom they trust, they do not fear sharing their opinions, debating the validation of others, and standing up for their own points of view. However, when it comes to conflict there is no lack of blind spots waiting to showcase you as something different than what you truly are.

What is Conflict?

According to Merriam Webster, conflict is defined as, "to be different, opposed, or contradictory; to fail to be in agreement or accord."

Conflict occurs when we think we are always right and those who disagree with us are wrong. Examples include, not listening to others, always coming up with reasons the ideas of others won't work, devaluing other's ideas, arguing with anyone who disagrees with you, refusing to explore other options, making assumptions on others intent or their ideas.

Growing up, I constantly felt I had to prove myself as an immigrant to Canada, which is why I developed conflict as one of my blind spots. Being an immigrant, I barely spoke English and had difficulty learning to write. I was bullied, taunted, and felt the constant need to prove myself to others. This blind spot carried with me into my business and how I interacted with my employees. I became a perfectionist in everything I did and nothing less was acceptable.

This attitude created conflict with my employees because I only had one point of view - mine. I didn't allow room for engagement nor did I create a space for employees to feel safe in contributing their point of view or ideas.

I worked extra hard to make sure my personal success was measured by how well I did in my business. However, I also lost sight that personal success also means how many lives you can empower and motivate people to rise up to be their best, which means sometimes you have to listen to others. I had to make room for healthy conflict so any existing roadblocks between myself and my employees were removed.

There only exists room for commitment to getting the job done and moving forward as an entire team. The success of any company is not built by just one person, but by an entire team of people willing to overcome conflict and commit to getting the results needed.

I recall a migration project for a client. In the IT industry, a migration project to a cloud server was not an easy task back then. A lot of preparation, documenting, following the process, and collaboration needs to occur. It's not a one-man effort and usually requires more than one person on the project. Since I wanted to prove I could do the project with a quick turn-around time, I made sure my employees understood that as well. I received some objections from my technical team on this unrealistic expectation, but I was adamant in showcasing our abilities to this new client and I refused to hear their frustrations and stress. As you can imagine, communication lines broke down, conflict started to arise as a result, and the project became a nightmare.

When I look back, I can see how I created the conflict. I didn't trust my team and didn't provide the opportunity to listen to them. In turn they felt unsafe and as the project commenced, they withheld communication from me when they were facing challenges because they felt I was unapproachable. Funny thing about conflict – if you don't have trust all around, people can't engage in healthy conflict dialogue and this issue rears its ugly head when issues start to arise or when goals/projects can't be completed.

After this disaster, I realized the issue was my conflict blind spot. When I had to own up to my employees that my leadership behavior caused the conflict and their inability to perform their work effectively, was when I started to change. Part of developing leadership model-ling behaviors is in recognizing the impact of actions and behaviors on others and the business. There is no shame. It takes a lot of courage and vulnerability in leadership to model the right behaviors and move an organization forward towards high performing results.

Conflict Bind Spot Behaviour

We behave in certain ways when we don't trust the people we interact with, which affects our ability to succeed. Leaders who don't trust their teams will create toxic environments by breeding conflict in others inside and outside of the team. Here are some of the be-haviours that conflict creates in people:

In Sales:

We've all met the type of salesperson who thrives in conflict. They walk into your office and quickly take control. Before you know it, they have jumped into their presentation telling you what you need and why he's the guy to get it for you. You barely get a word in edge-wise as he spouts off all the great reasons you need to buy from him. When you ask how much, he doesn't answer but keeps telling you how wonderful he and the company he works for are. Then when he hits you with the price, he's ready to do battle and loves negotiating a good deal for himself. You try to tell him "no", but he won't hear of it and begins to manipulate you into signing on the dotted line.

In Leadership:

A manager with a conflict blind spot will do one of two things, avoid it at all costs or be constantly demanding more from his team. A manager who avoids conflict will try to keep everyone happy but won't succeed and the team will feel unheard and on their own to solve their issues with the work, the client, or each other. The manager who uses conflict to bully his team into seeing things his way will not listen to the team or provide them with a safe place to discuss their limitations and weaknesses. It's his way or the highway.

In Service:

Customer Service Reps live with conflict every day as people come to them with problems, complaints, and issues. They have to be masters at diffusing conflict situations and communication. Too often an organization does not give its service department the tools to fix conflicts and when this happens, customers will go elsewhere. On the other side of conflict, customer service policies which avoid conflict will give away too much to a customer to make sure they are happy, and this affects the businesses bottom line as customers start to take advantage.

Conflict is a normal and natural occurrence of interacting with one another. The cost of resolving conflict is negligible relative to the cost of leaving conflicts unresolved. Difficult behavior can inhibit performance in others and will only deteriorate if left alone, contaminating more people and incurring hidden costs for the organization. It takes many forms like rudeness, yelling, shunning, mobbing, gossiping, refusing to talk to or acknowledge others, harassing, incessant complaining to supervisors, ignoring directives, and slow working.

FOCUS ON INTERESTS NOT POSITIONS . . .

A basic problem in communication lies not so much in conflicting positions, but in the conflict between each person's needs, desires, concerns, and fears. One person may say to another, "You're such a perfectionist in everything you do around here, and I'm tired of you thinking you're always right." That position is something the speaker has decided upon, but the interest is what caused that decision. The underlying interest might be a lack of training and a fear of competition with a skilled co-worker. The other person may not knowingly be competing but merely trying to do a good job, but the perception enables the conflict. Interests motivate people and are the silent movers behind the hubbub of positions.

WHY IS LISTENING SO IMPORTANT . . .

Listening is an art by which we use empathy to reach across the space between us. Passive attention doesn't work. Not only is listening an active process, it also often takes a deliberate effort to suspend our own needs and reactions. To listen well you must hold back what you have to say and control the urge to interrupt or argue. The art of listening requires a submersion of the self and immersion in the other. This is not always easy, especially when we are interested but too concerned with controlling or instructing or reforming the other person to be truly open to their point of view.

Conflict resolution is frequently one of the most challenging aspects of team leadership. Here are some of the ways team members can help manage conflicts:

- Listen with empathy and respect
- Allow others to express their concerns
- Look deeper, beyond what is being said, to understand the real meaning

- Be self-reflective and accountable—acknowledge if you are at fault
- Express emotions in a positive way—to encourage understanding and conflict resolution
- Prioritize—try to separate what is important and what gets in the way of understanding
- Learn from difficult behaviours —use what you have observed to see if outcomes have been affected

Good leaders, recognize that conflict:
- Doesn't need to be destructive.
- Should be leveraged rather than "managed" or "controlled."
- Can be handled with compassion.

Taking a compassionate approach could mean more— but healthier—conflict. Give the other person ownership in the resolution. Don't sell your ideas but engage in a joint problem-solving discussion. Ask what's important and be sure agreement is reached in respect for each of you.

Ask Yourself in Hindsight

Deep Dive

In this part of the book you are given lots of space to write, doodle, and draw, to understand your level of trust and those who trust you. This isn't a test. I will never see your answers, and neither will anyone else if you don't want them to. This exercise and all the other exercises in this book are meant only for you. This is your truth. If you want to discover your truth, then you must be 100% honest with yourself.

The questions are meant to get your mind thinking about behaviors, blind spots, and trust from different points of view. Whether you write the words, doodle images, or draw pictures to get your truth out on paper is up to you. Perhaps you want to record your answers using an app on your phone or computer and then play the answers back to yourself. There are a number of ways for you to answer these questions, use the method which works best for you.

Checklist A

- [ ] Avoid conflict
- [ ] Communication is one direction
- [ ] Don't value the contributions of team members
- [ ] Blame others, circumstances, and processes for failures
- [ ] Control of information, tasks, and won't share with others
- [ ] Fail to keep your promises, agreements and commitments
- [ ] Micromanage and resist delegating.
- [ ] Inconsistency between what you say and how you behave
- [ ] Scapegoating others
- [ ] Judge blame and criticize rather than offer feedback
- [ ] Do not allow others to contribute or make decisions
- [ ] Refuse to compromise to foster win-lose arguments
- [ ] Refuse to be held accountable by your colleagues.
- [ ] Don't discuss your personal life
- [ ] Aren't vulnerable
- [ ] Don't ask colleagues for help
- [ ] Take suggestions and critiques as personal attacks
- [ ] Refuse to follow through on decisions
- [ ] Secret back-door negotiations to create alliances
- [ ] Refuse to apologize

Checklist B

- [ ] Are Transparent with intentions
- [ ] Say what they mean and mean what they say
- [ ] Asks for team member input & feedback
- [ ] Understands failures are part of the process not a fault
- [ ] Is a resource of information for others to go to
- [ ] Can count on them to get the job done
- [ ] Enables teammates to do their job
- [ ] What you see is what you get
- [ ] Takes responsibility for actions
- [ ] Gives constructive feedback
- [ ] Supports teammates
- [ ] Negotiates to ensure win-win
- [ ] Mediates conflict
- [ ] Shares appropriate personal stories
- [ ] Are vulnerable
- [ ] Asks for help
- [ ] Focused on solutions not problems
- [ ] Apologizes for mistakes
- [ ] Acts for the good of the team
- [ ] People trust them

If checklist A, you need help. Your team may be engaging in negative conflict behaviour with each other and are not working together to meet your organization's objectives.

If checklist B, you have a team who engages in positive conflict behaviours to work together to move towards your team's objectives.

If checklist A & B are approximately equal, you have a team of mixed conflict behaviours, which is impeding your team's overall success. You will need to work with them to build healthy conflict discussions.

Go back and make a list of those behaviours from Checklist A, which you will need to be aware of, and find solutions to move team members from negative conflict to positive conflict.

Ask yourself

Following are a number of questions with space for you to place your answers to help you redefine your team and yourself to be more trusting and supportive of each other.

What is one thing your team can do differently to improve its conflict discussions?

How does your team use conflict?

_____

_____

_____

_____

Do all team members contribute ideas? Who doesn't?

_____

_____

_____

_____

Do you often find yourself needing to be in control?

_____

_____

_____

_____

Do you feel your team doesn't tell you necessary information?

_____

_____

_____

Conflict Deep Dive

Sometimes you engage in conflict without fear or malice. Other times you avoid conflict or you jump into it with the intent to win at all costs. Take the time to dive into your relationship with conflict to understand how you portray yourself during an altercation and when you engage in healthy conflict to advance an idea or project.

Did you witness your parents engage in healthy debates? What can you remember about these conversations?

Did you witness your parents fight or engage in unhealthy conflict? What do you remember about these moments in your life?

When you got in trouble as a child, how did your parents communicate with you? Describe a time you remember getting into trouble and explain how you felt.

Did you feel heard as a child? Or were you expected to do what you were told? Did you feel your voice was ignored, dismissed, or belittled?

Why was conflict easy or difficult for you as a child?

Think about the last conflict you were engaged in, what type of conflict was it? Difference of opinion, healthy debate of an idea, or an emotionally charged disagreement?

Did you want to have the conversation?

How did you feel before?

How did you feel during?

How did you feel after?

Did you feel heard during the conversation?

How do you think they felt before the conflict?

How do you think they felt during the conflict?

How do you think they felt after the conflict?

Did you think they felt heard during the conversation?

Think about how those who make you feel safe during conflict behave towards you. What do they do to make you feel safe to voice
your opinion?

How could you behave in order to allow them to be more open and
honest with you during a conflict situation to make it more productive?

Always strive for Excellence. I value excellence in my life and in my work and expect it from those on my team. Excellence doesn't mean perfection. It doesn't mean you will never make a mistake.

Excellence is the striving to be the best version of yourself and to deliver your best work consistently.

Sure you'll make mistakes. You'll stumble and make bad decisions. That doesn't matter, what matters is what you do afterwards... Will you strive for excellence or shrug and push the problem off on someone else?

Limiting Beliefs
Created by Conflict

Limiting Beliefs

Before we look forward, we have to look back and understand our limiting beliefs and where they came from so we can move forward.

We all have these stories from our childhood. Words that were meant to inspire us resulted in limiting beliefs and hurt feelings. When we fail, we point to those times and say, "There is the evidence," instead of seeing the reality of the situation. I've met people who are drowning in the evidence of their lack of worth and inability to succeed because instead of seeing their skills and talents, they point to the evidence of why they are where they are in life. For them, the "You aren't going to amount to anything" comment is said a thousand different ways throughout their lives by those who love them, know them, and hold positions of power in their lives. They do not lack evidence to limit them.

Blind Spot behaviours draw from this well of low expectations, limiting comments, and criticisms as automatic responses to perceived threats.

Think back on the events in your life and make a list of all the times someone caused you pain, loss, and isolation.

What happened?

Who was involved?

How did you feel?

What is this event evidence of?

"Do not allow your fire to go out, spark by irreplaceable spark in the hopeless swamps of the not-quite, the not-yet, and the not at all. Do not let the hero in your soul perish in lonely frustration for the life you deserved and have never been able to reach. The world you desire can be won. It exists. It is real. It is possible. It is yours.

" Ayn Rand

On this page continue listing the evidence limiting your success.

For example:

I'm not good enough because my mom criticized everything I ever did.

I don't get along with others because I have no friends.

I am unlovable because I can't find someone to love me.
I am unemployable because no one will hire me.

Take a moment to think about how your behaviours are protecting you from being victimized again.

For every event which provides evidence of your limiting belief, write down what behaviours you exhibit to protect yourself from reliving the negative emotions of your past.

What is the limiting belief?

_____

_____

_____

_____

How do you behave to protect yourself?

_____

_____

_____

_____

How do you want to behave instead?

_____

_____

_____

_____

What is the limiting belief?

How do you behave to protect yourself?

How do you want to behave instead?

In your journal complete this exercise for each limiting belief you have and the evidence your mind has collected as proof these siblings went through the same thing and say it was nothing. It is a fact of life that siblings turn out differently though they shared a number of the same experiences. It is common for people to go through the same experience and for one person, the event had no effect, whereas the other is left traumatized. How you are affected by the actions and words of others depends on your personality, self-esteem, and support system. There are no wrong answers in this exercise, your experiences and feelings matter.

The Other Side

When lawyers argue a case in court, they choose what to bring into evidence to back up their argument. They do their best to negate evidence which does not fit their theories by offering more compelling evidence to support their point of view. In the next exercise you are going to take on the persona of a lawyer to argue your case and bring forth evidence to back up your argument.

For example:

Limiting / negative belief:

I am not worth $X Opposing argument: I am worth $X

The evidence supporting the opposing statement:

I have a degree in X

I have X number of happy clients

I work hard to produce a high-quality product

I have a client testimonial saying X

I completed project X with X results

I have #X of years of experience

I possess experience at X

I have the following skills:

I have the following talents:

If you have a hard time finding evidence, it is time to ask others for help. A lot of people are buried by negative evidence from a lifetime of abuse, criticism, failure, and rejection. Though these things affect us, they are not the truth of who you are, what you can do, or what you deserve in life. They are the result of how your behaviours have been interpreted by those around you. It is also the result of how you interpret their behaviours, off-hand comments, and knee jerk reactions to your behaviour. There is a lot of room for misunderstandings and miscommunication when you try to interpret what others think about you.

New Case Evidence

The behaviours and words of others have built a case against you in your mind, it is time to find out what people really think about you. You can do a number of things to discover evidence to back up your new argument.

1. Brainstorm with your team for work related arguments.
2. Send out requests for testimonials / reviews to clients.
3. Take a look at your competitor's work and how it compares to yours.
4. Ask a friend if they believe you are X and why.
5. Ask family members if they believe you are X and why.

If you are able to and are brave enough to, you can ask those who provided you evidence for your negative beliefs if they really meant X, and would they still agree or disagree with that statement now? If you don't feel brave enough to face them and ask, you can email or text the question to them.

But what if they really do believe the negative stuff about me? Good question! By asking, one of two things will happen. Either they will negate their previous evidence and provide you with evidence for your new argument, or they will say they agree with the original judgement. If they provide you with new evidence, you will be better off and your relationship with them will grow. If they believe the original judgement, you will know, and can proceed to cut them off or limit the amount of influence they have in your life, if you so choose. Do you want people in your life who are not supportive? It may be time to make room for new people in your life.

Discover the Evidence

What is the original limiting belief argument?

_____

_____

_____

_____

What is the new opposing argument?

_____

_____

_____

_____

_____

Discover the Evidence for the opposing argument:

_____

_____

_____

_____

Continue this exercise for every limiting belief you have in a journal until you have enough evidence to negate your limiting beliefs.

What if I discover the limiting belief is correct because there is no evidence to the contrary?

Good question. There may be some beliefs where you need to do the work to build evidence against the belief. Maybe you need to go back to school to get certified. Perhaps you are short on experience so you need to volunteer or help someone to gain the experience you need to prove you can do the job. These are things you can do to overcome certain obstacles to getting to where you want to be in life.

These are only obstacles. Things you can overcome because you have the ability to do what is necessary to succeed. If you need to take a course, you have skills and natural talents to complete the course. If you need experience, you have a skillset to ensure you will succeed and build your reputation.

Make a list of your natural talents and skills. Beside each one, write the obstacle you will use that skill or talent to overcome.

For example:

Can read
Can take course X
Passionate about X
Course will be fun
Natural talent X
Can get good grade for course
Hard Working X
Can do the work to get course
Go getter

Achieve the goal

Make a list of your skills, talents, and abilities, and how they will help you to overcome the obstacles in the way of getting the evidence you need for your new belief system.

Matrix
Committed

Matrix Committed

"Objectives are not fate; they are direction. They are not commands; they are commitments. They do not determine the future; they are means to mobilize the resources and energies of the business for the making of the future."
Peter Drucker

To be committed to your business you have to ask the right questions and trust the process. When you commit to the process you show that you are focused on the results. Unfortunately, after I brought people into Matrix, I didn't trust the process or the plan, and was not focused on the result.

I would create a marketing/sales plan or an operations plan to ensure we had KPIs to measure to ensure everyone was doing the job they were committed to doing. Then, my scarcity mindset would stoke my fear of not having enough and I'd go looking for a better way, a better process, and we'd be off on a tangent which had nothing to do with the original goal.

When Matrix was just me, the focus was on client relationships and making sure I was helping them keep their computer networks operational so they could be productive. The process was based on asking questions, understanding the client's needs, and providing the service to solve their problems. Since I wasn't committed to the process, it was easy for me to change course.

In 2010 I hired a marketing company who suggested I grow and increase my business tenfold by bringing people into Matrix. I agreed to change the course of my business because on paper, I'd make more money. My commitment changed from client focused relationships to money making transactions. With the increased costs of bringing people on, my scarcity blind spot got in the way and I made bad choices because I was scared of not having enough.

After I brought on new people, distrust and scarcity led me to abandon my original goal and focus. Now, my focus was on the transactions to ensure my staff was doing the job I was paying them for. I limited the amount of exposure they had with our clients because I was scared they would steal my customers and go off to start their own firm. I should have been focused on the client, not on my staff, and I should have been mentoring my staff with the goal of helping them go out on their own. This is one of my biggest regrets because the people I had hired were talented and capable IT professionals. We could have changed the way IT worked with clients but distrust and scarcity got in the way.

To do this, I needed to trust my staff and my staff needed to be empowered to contribute to the process so they would commit to it, own it, and focus on the result instead of the task. I had demanded they clear a certain number of tickets every day and then pushed them to meet that number. To meet that number, they didn't take the time to ask the necessary questions to understand the real problem. By fixing the symptom, the problem came back as a new ticket the next day and suddenly the number of tickets grew exponentially. The switch from commitment to the client relationship to the commitment to clearing the tickets resulted in more problems.

I reacted to this problem by focusing on the symptom; an increase in daily tickets instead of finding the solution to the real problem. Had I taken the time to step back and look at what was really happening, I would have understood the problem was that we were no longer focused on the client relationships.

With my frustration increasing, I searched for quick fix ideas and implemented new ways to motivate staff and new ways to get the job done, however, I did not commit to any of these new ideas long enough for them to make a difference. I wanted results right away because of scarcity and when I didn't get the improved result, I'd find a new idea to get the results I wanted. I was going from one hamster wheel to another and going backwards instead of forwards.

Since I had personal responsibilities which I was committed to: my wife, my kids, a mortgage, and a lifestyle we'd all become accustomed to, I knew I needed to keep trying to find a solution. If the income from the business fell, I felt the pressure of my family's fear of scarcity and need for me to create wealth for our security. When my dad was alive, he was a successful businessman who gave us a good lifestyle because he'd built wealth which gave us the security we wanted. After he died, we lost that security and wealth as others came in to take it over, pushing us out of the business ownership. His death had a far reaching impact on both his sons. His death, I felt, had left me with scarcity, fear of not being enough, not having enough, and distrusting everyone who could take it away.

Staying focused on the result means you have to know what result you truly want and what it looks, feels, and sounds like. It has to be real to you and trusting the daily tasks of your process will lead you to that result. You also have to commit to doing the work every day and to stay on track without chasing every new idea that crosses your path.

When you have a new idea or learn a new tactic, weigh it against the result you want to see. If it will help you achieve that result, implement it. If not, let it go and stay committed to your goals.

Avoiding Commitment

What is Commitment?

According to Webster's dictionary, commitment is an agreement or pledge to do something in the future. Pledging resources to something. The state or an instance of being obligated or emotionally impelled to do something.

A lack of commitment can occur when you treat your promises casual. If it gets done it gets done, if it's late, it's late, we'll get it done when we do. It can show up in a lack of emotional commitment because you don't believe in the project, your heart isn't in it, or you are not fully engaged in seeing things through to the end result. Sometimes, a lack of commitment comes across as wishy washy because you don't take a stand for what you believe, or you don't really care either way. All of these behaviours and attitudes can be attributed to the lack of commitment blind spot, which will impede your success and that of your team.

When people aren't committed to anything, it can mean they were not held accountable in the past so they do not believe it matters if they keep their word, deliver on time, or show up. In business, a lack of commitment happens because the right questions haven't been asked due to not trusting the process.

When I read Robin Sharma's book, the 5am Club, I decided to commit to the process. In the book he says, "Own your morning, elevate your life." The idea is to get up at five and do 20 minutes of cardio, 20 minutes of reflection, meditation, or journaling, and 20 minutes of personal development. Doing these activities first thing in the morning gets you in the right mindset to take on your day. You start at 5 because the hours of four to six are the most peaceful hours. I committed to this morning routine on December 24 of 2018 for six months and my life changed. I credit my commitment to this process to the positive changes in my life during 2019. I discovered what I wanted out of life and where I wanted my business to go. Every day I committed to everything I said I was going to do, including courses on public speaking to become a professional speaker.

And then life got in the way.

At first, I was committed to the 5 am club. Then it became the 7am Club. Then, only when I felt like it, and my personal development stagnated. My business stagnated. I wasn't going through the process and my results reflected my lack of commitment. I recommitted to the 5am club January 2020 and found my drive, motivation, and opportunities. I'm committed to growth and personal development and it's made a difference in my life, but I had to commit to myself.

"Anyone can become an everyday leader by showing up as I'm encouraging. When it's easy and especially when it's difficult. Starting today, and if you do so, a guaranteed victory is in your future. And I need to add that there is not one person alive today who cannot lift their thinking, performance, vitality, prosperity and lifetime happiness magnificently by writing in a series of profound daily rituals and then practicing them until they become your second nature."

OWN YOUR MORNING, ELEVATE YOUR LIFE.
- Robin Sharma 5am Club

The first step to positive change is a commitment to yourself. You have to commit to creating the life you want. A mentor I look up to has helped me to get where I am today. He helped me to work on this exercise called life, which is designed by us.

I get teared up every time I talk about this change in my life because I tried to make changes throughout my life but wasn't able to achieve the results I wanted. For example, I tried losing weight through different diets and I didn't achieve long term results. Then I met my mentor and we started talking about creating the life I wanted.

He asked me what the life I wanted looked like? I didn't understand what it looked like, what I wanted. I went to a personal development seminar for professionals one day and the facilitator asked what we wanted. Everyone stood up to explain what they wanted for their businesses, careers, and professions. The Lululemon staff were there and when it was my turn I stood up and said, "I want my company to be like Lululemon because they're so engaged, and they love everybody. Look at you guys. You are all here." Then I sat down and didn't think about my answer.

During the next break a Lululemon manager came over and asked me, "What did you mean when you said you want to be like Lululemon?" I said, "I like the way you guys are, your culture." She then asked if she could come by my office the next day to go through an exercise with my team. Of course, I invited her to visit. She had one condition, for all the members of my team to be committed to doing the exercise. "No problem."

My whole team showed up the next day and agreed to participate in the exercise. She gave us some paper and pens before asking us, "How do you want to feel in 10 years?" Where are you going to be? Where are you going to wake up? Who are you going to wake up with? What are you going to be wearing? What are you going to be smelling? What will your day look like?"

At first, I created a checklist which basically was a list of my present life, but better. That wasn't what she wanted. She was asking us to write a story full of emotion and details, one we could see in our minds. It is easier to commit to a future life when it is a story full of emotions and details than a sterile checklist. That was 7 years ago, and I am 80% closer to the life I dreamed of that day.

In Sales:

Commission sales staff who are not committed to the process, the position, or the company are distracted. They are late for meetings. They have inconsistent results and spend more time looking busy than being productive. They have 2-hour martini lunches, stop working early most days, and at noon on Fridays. They miss their quotas or barely meet them by bringing in sales at the end of the month. They will promise customers anything but can't be bothered to follow through. They live by doing what they want, hitting the easy button, and handing in paperwork full of errors. They do not strive for excellence.

In Leadership:

Leaders who aren't committed are easily distracted and led astray. They do not communicate clearly because they are balancing on a fence, trying to keep the peace to make everyone happy. They are more concerned with their own careers, goals, and desires than what is best for the team or the organization. A leader who is not committed is always looking for the next opportunity for themselves instead of producing the best results for the one they have.

When team members are unwilling to weigh in and share their opinions, they are not going to commit to whatever decision is made. A team which fails to commit, creates ambiguity amongst the team about directions and priorities. They will miss opportunities due to excessive analysis and indecisiveness, which breeds a lack of confidence and a fear of failure. They may reverse their discussions by constantly changing their minds or second guessing themselves. A clear sign of this is if a team continues to talk about the same issues over and over because they are not committed to the process they previously agreed to or didn't have an honest conversation about the core issue.

To develop commitment in your team, you will need to communicate clearly, engage everyone, and ensure you have discussed the real problem to come up with the right solutions for your team. By developing a process, you will create boundaries and as you create boundaries you will define consequences to encourage commitment. The key is to commit to the boundaries as a leader to be clear about your expectations and the reasons why tasks must be done within the agreed timeframe. If you do not commit to the boundary, your team will not commit to the process because if you don't care that they don't meet their commitments, they won't.

Organizations aren't succeeding because they are not committing to the process, the KPIs, or the desired results. To ensure your team is committed to drive the organization forward, you need to communicate why you are asking them to do certain tasks. If you realize there is a lack of commitment on your team you need to first determine what you want the result to be and what you want them to commit to. Have you discussed with your team what commitment looks like and why it is important to ensure the result you are working towards?

For example, if an automotive sales manager wants to increase sales next month, he will ask his sales team to increase the tasks which lead to sales. He may say, "Call 10 prospects a day to go for a test drive in the new SUV." The sales team starts calling 10 prospects a day to increase test drives, but the sale won't happen because the pitch was to come for a test drive, not buy the car. Now, if the sales manager said, "Reach out to 10 people to see what their transportation needs are and communicate how we can help them meet those needs," then you're committing to the process of helping people solve their transportation problem, not selling them a test drive. This process will help the salesperson understand why the potential client wants to buy a vehicle. When the salespeople understand their job is uncovering the client's why and not just trying to sell them a test drive, they will trust the process because they understand why they are doing it. When they trust the process, they will commit to it.

A lot of people feel commitments are KPIs, numbers and tasks that are easily measured in numbers. However, a commitment happens when people understand the reasons, they need to do the tasks you've asked them to do. If a person understands we have to get an email out to 4000 people by June 1st to give them five days to RSVP for the event on June 6th, then the team member now understands that if she doesn't get the email out by June 1st, it will affect the result. If she doesn't complete her part, then the whole project is affected. There is a clear commitment, reason, and consequence. If the team member does not believe sending out emails to 4000 people matters to the end result, she may miss the June 1st deadline or send the wrong message in the email because she did not understand its purpose. There must be buy-in and understanding about why the task matters.

Ask team members, "Do you know why we are doing the project and what end result we want?" Don't tell them, ask them so you know they understand and get buy-in from them when they explain it in their own words. If they don't know the answer, have a conversation about the project, what it is, and why the team is doing it. You have to be willing to go back to trust and conflict conversations to build the team's commitment.

Let's say we're running a track and field baton race. If I kind of give you the baton, are you going to be able to grab it and run your leg of the race? You'll probably drop it or engage in a bit of a tug of war. If I trust you and know you are committed to getting the baton across the finish line, I'll let go as I pass it to you because I trust you will grab hold of it and run with it. If your team is committed to the end result, you will know the results your team wanted will be achieved.

Teams who demonstrate a lack of commitment to their goal breed a lack of confidence and a fear of failure, which results with inaction and indecision. When a team member is not committed to the results, they will cause friction, delays, and second guessing, by constantly questioning the process and direction the team is going. They will reanalyze and debate initiatives without taking action or producing solutions. This results in animosity, as members of the team who are committed and accountable feel resentment toward those who don't pull their weight. People think, "Why am I doing so much more than this person? If this is the level of commitment that's expected, then I can dial my commitment back to match." This, in turn, can drag the whole team down and derail any positive progress toward achieving results.

In Service:

The commitment will only happen in the customer service if they understand what they're committing to. It is easy to put numbers on the customer service department to increase efficiency however you can't quantify relationship building through numbers. In the technology industry, we used to have to close 25 tickets a day. The team committed to the task and closed 25 tickets a day. However, the next day we opened up 30 because 20 of them were done wrong. They were given the wrong commitment. The commitment needed to be to bring success to 25 clients today to ensure the real problem is solved. This way, the team took the time to understand the core of the problem, what the customer needed, and completed the tasks to provide the right solution.

Commitment isn't about consensus – it's about leaving behind ambiguity to bring about a solid course of action.

Ask Yourself in Hindsight

Deep Dive

In this part of the book you are given lots of space to write, doodle, draw, to understand your level of trust and those who trust you. This isn't a test. I will never see your answers, neither will anyone else if you don't want them to. This exercise and all the other exercises in this book are meant only for you. This is your truth. If you want to discover your truth, then you must be 100% honest with yourself.

The questions are meant to get your mind thinking about behaviour, blind spots, and trust from different points of view. Whether you write the words, doodle images, or draw pictures to get your truth out on paper is up to you. Perhaps you want to record your answers using an app on your phone or computer and then play the answers back to yourself. There are a number of ways for you to answer these questions. Use the method which works best for you.

Checklist A

- ☐ Uses hedging language
- ☐ Refuse to give a clear yes or no
- ☐ Avoids committing to a specific date or deadline
- ☐ Makes promises but does not deliver
- ☐ Avoids being held accountable
- ☐ Talks a good game but has no actions to back it up
- ☐ Lack of follow-through
- ☐ Resists making an authentic commitment
- ☐ Complies and goes along to get along
- ☐ Isn't enthusiastic
- ☐ Has a wait and see attitude
- ☐ Resigned to the status quo - nothing will change
- ☐ People don't know what they stand for
- ☐ Publically agrees but doesn't provide real support
- ☐ Revisits the same topic over and over
- ☐ Takes a long time to make a decision or won't make one
- ☐ Lack of a clear position on most topics
- ☐ Changes their mind often are seen as wishy washy
- ☐ Tolerates indecisiveness
- ☐ Risk adverse

Checklist B

- [ ] Knows what they want
- [ ] Say what they mean and mean what they say
- [ ] Has a track record for completing tasks on time
- [ ] Takes calculated risks to ensure results are delivered
- [ ] Meets deadlines and KPIs consistently
- [ ] Can count on them to get the job done
- [ ] Decisive
- [ ] What you see is what you get
- [ ] Takes responsibility for actions
- [ ] Know where the person stands on an issue
- [ ] Makes his opinions known and supports teammates
- [ ] Negotiates to ensure win-win
- [ ] Mediates conflict
- [ ] Will take responsibility for mistakes
- [ ] Is enthusiastic
- [ ] Asks for help
- [ ] Focused on solutions not problems
- [ ] Participates in discussions
- [ ] Acts for the good of the team
- [ ] People trust them

If checklist A: you need help. Your team may be engaging in negative conflict behaviour with each other and are not working together to meet your organization's objectives.

If checklist B, you have a team who engages in positive conflict behaviours to work together to move towards your team's objectives.

If checklist A & B are approx. equal, you have a team of mixed conflict behaviours, which is impeding your team's overall success. You will need to work with your team to build healthy conflict discussions.

Go back and make a list of those behaviours from Checklist A, which you will need to be aware of and find solutions to in order to move team members from negative conflict to positive conflict.

Ask yourself

Following are a number of questions with space for you to place your answers to help you redefine your team and yourself to be more trusting and supportive of each other.

Do you make promises but conveniently leave out when something is going to happen?

Do you delay making decisions or avoid making them altogether? Is your team performing to their potential?

How does a lack of commitment affect your team? Either your lack of commitment or a member of the team.
Are you meeting deadlines?

Does your leaders bring work to your team because they know you will get it done?

When your team didn't commit to a project, what was the reason and how could you have inspired them to commit?

What does the word commitment mean to you?

Describe what it looks like to be committed:

In work?

In Leadership?

In Friendship?

In Family?

In a Relationship?

What do you need to see from your team members to know they are committed to results?

What do you need to see from leadership to know they are committed to results?

What results do you want your team to achieve?

What do they need to do every day to achieve these results?

How can you clearly communicate the results you want while ensuring they are doing the daily tasks to meet those results?

"For businesses to excel they need to search for organizational and personal blind spots because they are the underlying reasons, we can't have authentic connections with people. They are the reason we struggle to find our purpose and passion in life. Why we don't have a clear focus to get the outcomes we want in our work and our lives.

Getting to the source of what's driving our behaviors requires vulnerability and a willingness to accept how we show up to others, which can be uncomfortable. Especially, if we are not ready to accept our flaws and faults.

Leaders have a responsibility to become aware of their blind spots because others rely on them to lead the organization to successful outcomes. Thing is, even if the leader cannot see their own blind spots, those around him do see them.

Matrix in Integrity

Matrix

Integrity is important to me and I commit to living in it every day. It shows up in everything we do. If you don't honor somebody, you don't honor yourself. Being on time is important to me because I believe showing up when you say shows respect for others. If you can't show up when you say you were going to, it says you believe your time is more important than the other person.

Once you start believing you are more important than others, you will start treating people without respect and make excuses for yourself which you would not allow others to make. Earlier, I shared how one of my employees showed up 10 minutes late to the weekly meeting. I wouldn't be in integrity if I always allowed him to be late. So, one day I pointed out to him that he'd just wasted 100 minutes of his team's time and I couldn't afford to pay for 100 minutes of unproductive time. I told him if he was going to be late he should not attend. He was late for the next meeting and I stayed in integrity by telling him to leave. He was never late again.

If you don't show up on time to a meeting, you probably don't show up on time for a party or to a friend's house for dinner. There's a negative impact of stress being put on yourself because you're late, so you're driving fast. You're not checking for your blind spots, you go fast and drive dangerously. Committing to being true to your word is only the beginning of living in integrity, the rest is in everything we do. I believe if you're going to do something, you need to do it with excellence. The Matrix team needed to be a High Performance Team to be successful, Anything less would keep us from meeting our goals.

How we do anything is how we do everything.

For example, imagine a racing team. Everyone on the team works hard to get the car ready for the race. They work fast in the pit to ensure the driver has a top performing car to cross the finish line. Then the driver gets in the car and doesn't feel like being there, so he leisurely drives around the racetrack and casually finishes the race. He finishes the race but he won't be excellent and he will have let the rest of his team down. He didn't respect the effort they'd put in for him and as a result, the reward wasn't awarded. I knew my staff would either show up and be high performers or they would just show up to get a paycheck.

At Matrix, I had zero tolerance for not being excellent. A lot of people thought I meant they were in trouble if they made a mistake and would try to hide errors, make excuses, or point the blame at someone else. But that's not what I said. I didn't say they weren't allowed to make mistakes. I had zero tolerance for not being excellent.

Excellence meant doing their best by putting in 110% effort at work. I expected they would make mistakes. I was good with mistakes as long as they took responsibility for them, did their best to fix them, and communicated with the client to ensure the client relationship was strong. To be excellent, they needed to do their best at all times to deliver high quality service to our clients. They needed to be excellent in their communication, integrity, and taking care of customers all the time. If they couldn't play that level of game; the excellence game, then they weren't part of the team.

It was that simple.

I had little tolerance for unproductive behaviours while at work. This included gossiping, which is destructive to morale, wastes time, and is not in integrity. If you are going to put others down, spread rumours and lies to make yourself look or feel better, then you are not treating people the way you want to be treated. In order to be living in integrity it is important to act the way you want others to act. To ensure team members could live in integrity with each other it was important I hired people who shared similar core values.

At first, I didn't hire people based on their values or how they would fit within the culture of the office. I hired based on who applied and if they had the certification. As you can imagine, it created problems and my front door became a revolving door of staff. These were skilled people who couldn't fit into the culture of excellence and integrity. Providing my clients with excellent service was vital to my success but not all clients are created equal.

To remain in integrity it is important to take on work with clients who hold the same values as you and have integrity themselves. When I took on new staff, I was open to bringing on any client I could and the result was an increased level of stress and problems. I was making decisions to take on any client because I was more concerned about the bottom dollar. My scarcity blind spot was driving my decisions, not my integrity. I didn't make sure the client would fit in with how I wanted to do business. Conflict, unreasonable demands, and unpaid bills became part of our day to day because I wanted to make money on each transaction instead of facilitating the building of relationships between my clients and my staff.

When I took on the added expense of hiring people, my financial compensation became smaller, but my financial needs remained high. My wife Sam became stressed about the bank balance and this caused my stress level to rise. I was scared of my financial future and kept pushing team members to produce, prospects to buy in, and clients to pay their invoices. My business changed because I was out of integrity and it made life difficult.

Integrity is about being congruent in your messaging and in who you are while also being true to the values you're committed to.

Picture a CEO who's been running a small company for a few decades. He's comfortable in his role at the top but has no idea how he is affecting the culture in his company.

One day, someone shines a light on his blind spots, and he wants to make a change and shift from getting to giving.

First, he becomes authentic and lets people see the real him, not the mask he's worn with his big title. He now shows his appreciation for his employees, through simple compliments and acknowledgement of work done well. Thanks to this new approach, he starts to see his employees acting differently.

Instead of hiding in their cubicles, they feel free to share ideas and make suggestions. Next, this CEO creates a positive influence by encouraging, guiding, and welcoming new ideas instead of criticizing and blocking employees by saying no.

He opens up to receiving feedback. He values his employees' opinions and welcomes them further by creating a culture of inclusion. Finally, he adds value to the whole company and their customers.

Living in Integrity

We'd like to believe people are simple and easy to under-stand – we aren't, we are complex. We all behave in different ways depending on the situation, the people, the time, our energy level, our mood, and hundreds of other variables. It is hard for people to really know each other until they spend a significant amount of time with them to determine who they really are because too often we aren't who we think we are.

Ever have someone tell you they were wonderful, had the right skills, was the perfect person for the job? Perhaps they tell you they are supportive, kind, and honest. Then something happens and their behaviours show a very different type of person. That person is nothing like who they said they were. Did they lie? Maybe.

If they lied, they probably lied to themselves first and be-lieved they were those things. However, when it comes down to it, they let others down. When this happens, they are not living in integrity. According to the Webster's dictionary, integrity is the qual-ity of being honest and having strong moral principles, moral up-rightness, or the state of being whole and undivided. This definition doesn't fully define integrity.

Integrity is doing what you say and committing to what you said. It's being congruent in your messages, being congruent in your values, staying true to yourself no matter the situation. It is also about being true to what you committed to as well as building relationships with people who are congruent to that integrity as well.

Integrity is the foundation for a successful employee-employer relationship. It promotes a culture where individuals can depend on one another because they treat each other with respect. As a result, people are typically more productive and motivated at work.

If I think about integrity, I think about holding people accountable to their words and actions. I used to have Monday meetings at Matrix, my IT company, at noon every week. It was an hour and a half long meeting about life by design and people hated it until they started realizing why we were doing it.

I wouldn't have a conversation with the consistently late employee about his tardiness because I didn't want to have a conflict and he was such a good employee otherwise. I didn't want to lose him because I knew he didn't like the meeting and wanted to rock the boat. I didn't push him. He kept on showing up late and then one day I confronted it.

After that, he always showed up on time. I had to make showing up on time important to him and everyone on the team.

This was a few years ago. He messaged me last year saying, "I wanted to reach out and let you know that you had a massive impact on my life. My time at Matrix turned a lot of things right for me. It led me to where I am today, and I couldn't be more thankful. I often think about how different things would have been if you guys had not brought me on the team." I didn't think he got it, but he got it. I believed in integrity and following up. If you say you're going to show up – show up.

Most people know what Ritz stands for. Excellent, excellent service.

I had the opportunity of staying there one night through a vendor, and I couldn't believe they knew my name when I walked up to the front desk. The staff had a print-out of a profile, including a picture of me, before I went in. They find you and now they have Google glasses to do facial recognition. It's not, "Hi, how are you?" It's "Hi, Mr. Lavji, Welcome to the Ritz Carlton. I hope your travels from Vancouver were good." It's an extra personal service.

There was a story about Ritz Carlton where a couple who went out one night were going on a cruise the next morning. The heel of the wife's shoe broke on their way back to the hotel late at night. When they passed the concierge hobbling, the attendant said, "Can I have your broken shoe? I'll have it resolved for you before you leave tomorrow morning on your cruise." He knew exactly who they were and that they were leaving the next morning on a cruise. He got the shoe fixed and dropped off at the room nicely wrapped and said, "Enjoy your trip." That is excellent service!

That's a different level, and when we get to that level, we can achieve excellence all the time. But what's stopping us from getting there? What blind spot is stopping you from living in integrity and being excellent?

Your blind spots affect every aspect of your life, how you show up in relationships, and how you react to others. Every single one of your actions causes either a positive or negative impact on others, who then react either positively or negatively towards you. This cycle can cause an issue to escalate out of control or an emotionally charged situation to explode. In a professional environment these reactions can impact a person's future opportunities for advancement and the team's effectiveness to succeed. As a leader, you will need the tools to understand the situation and how to defuse any negative emotional build up.

Living without Integrity

Here are some telltale behaviours of people who don't live in integrity.

In Sales:

We have all experienced the salesperson who promises us the moon and can't deliver the stratosphere. We call this over-promising and under-delivering. In some cases, the problem is with the support processes and operations of the company more than the salesperson and the company is not living in integrity.

The example of the salesperson who will say anything to get the sale, even if they know the company cannot deliver on the salesperson's promises, is one of integrity. When the product or service you received is less than they promised, while they still receive the commission, something is clearly out of alignment.

In Leadership:

Leaders who don't act with integrity will stretch the truth, spin the story, and pass the blame on to others. They will tell investors one story, while telling sales departments another, and service departments a third story. They make promises they know they cannot meet in order to get what they want and expect their teams to fix any issues which come up.

In Service:

How often have you called a service department of a large corporation to find out the company has no integrity because the person on the other end of the phone has no power to fix the issue? You find yourself lost in the call centre lottery over and over, hoping the next voice will have the power to help you. When a company structures its service department around making it difficult for customers to receive a resolution, the whole company is living outside of integrity.

When a service staff member is not living in integrity, they will promise anything, and say anything, to get you off the phone with no intention of doing the work to solve the problem. They will say they will call you at a certain time and you never hear from them again. They can fix the problem but it takes them too much effort or they forget to do it.

Living in Integrity

When we live in integrity, it shows, and everyone wins because the environment is one of collaboration, productivity, and account-ability. Leaders who lead with integrity are supportive, transparent, and trustworthy. Opportunity flows to those teams with integrity because they work together to get the job done.

In Sales:

When we live in integrity, we do what we say and we say what we know we can do. We create an environment where others feel they can ask for what they want because they believe we will deliver on our promises.

A salesperson who lives in integrity is more concerned with the relationship and wants to provide clients with solutions to meet their needs. They are more concerned with the customer's happiness than they are about the commission. If something goes wrong and their promise isn't being met, they will bend over backwards to solve the problem, even if it affects their commission. Doing what is right matters more to them than the pay cheque.

In Leadership:

When leaders act with integrity, they have open communica-tion, treat their teams with respect, and are consistent in their mes-saging with all departments and stakeholders. They understand the limits of their teams and work to help them find the resources they need to complete promises. Leaders who live in integrity are mindful of every word they say and ensure their behaviours match their words and their value systems.

In Service:

If the serviceperson has integrity, they will also do whatever they can to find out what happened and what solution they can provide. They will call you back because they said they would and if the company does not allow them to provide a satisfactory solution, they will offer to pass the issue on to someone who can fix it. Then they will follow up with that person to make sure the customer is being taken care of. Most large service call centres do not enable their service people to act in integrity, which results in terrible service all around.

We've all heard the saying, "Integrity is doing the right thing when no one is watching." This is only one aspect of integrity. Integrity is something people claim to possess or value in their lives, however, at times their actions do not align with their words. They are late for meetings. They do not follow through with projects or they forget tasks they promised they would do. These things may be seen as small and unimportant on their own, however, over time the disconnect between our behaviours and our words results in a blind spot which affects our success.

If you are consistently late for meetings or production deadlines, your co-workers, managers, and customers will begin to see you as unreliable. It does not matter that you finally finished the project if it's a month overdue and affected the productivity of other team members or teams. When they need someone to complete another project you may not be the person they choose because they do not trust you to complete the project in a timely manner.

Think about a time when someone told you they would do

something and they didn't. They might have forgotten, got too busy, or started to do it, but then abandoned the task as 'good enough.' When this happens how do you feel?

Integrity is a habit.

To live in integrity you must be mindful of what you say and take action to ensure what you say is what you do. If you cannot keep your word on the daily things, others will not trust you to work on the important things.

Think about the people in your life. Do you know someone who is known for always being late? What about a person who promises the moon and then disappears when it comes time to put in the work? How often has someone oversold you on a product or service and then under delivered?

The second part of integrity is delivering at the best of your ability regardless of circumstances. It means not cutting corners, or doing a half-assed job. It is about delivering consistent results which people can rely on.

We are human.

There are times when we fall and fail in our integrity for one reason or another. We are not perfect, nor should we expect perfection from others. We all make mistakes, but it is what we do afterwards which will determine if we continue to live in integrity or not.

Think about a time someone made a mistake which affected you negatively. How did they react? Did they fix the situation or did they pass blame onto someone else? Were you left holding the bag or did they provide you with a solution you could live with?

Integrity happens when you take responsibility for your actions and work to fix the situation. It is about making sure we step up so that others are not negatively affected by our mistakes. Making mistakes is not a bad thing, it is how we learn and grow. We can stay in integrity by communicating what went wrong and how we are going to fix it - then doing just that.

Tools to help us

If upon reflection you discover a disconnect between your words and your actions, you will need to find the tools to help you live in integrity. If you are always late for meetings, figure out why you are late. Do you get distracted by other things and lose track of the time? Do you forget to check your daily calendar to see what appointments you have that day? Are you constantly rushing from one appointment to the next with no idea why you are always late? Discover the reason you cannot live in integrity and seek out tools to help you to arrive early. Do you need to set an alarm on your phone so you know what time it is? Do you need a better calendar system which is more in tune with your working style? Do you need to understand how long it will take to get from one place to the next and then double the travel time into your calendar to account for traffic? Perhaps you need to learn how to say "No, that time doesn't work, how about this one?" Instead of always agreeing to other's timetables and ending up double booked.

There are lots of systems and tools available to help you manage your schedule and stay on track, so you can arrive early to meetings. Once you know the reason your behaviours and words are disconnected, you can then find the tool which will work best for your working style.

Integrity is a choice not a value. It is the consistent choosing to do the right thing when nobody's watching, to do what we say we are going to do, to deliver our best efforts, and to take responsibility for fixing our mistakes. Integrity is about choosing to be and do better than we did before.

Ask Yourself in Hindsight

Deep Dive

In this part of the book you are given lots of space to write, doodle, draw, to understand your level of trust and those who trust you. This isn't a test. I will never see your answers, neither will anyone else if you don't want them to. This exercise and all the other exercises in this book are meant only for you. This is your truth. If you want to discover your truth, then you must be 100% honest with yourself.

The questions are meant to get your mind thinking about behaviour, blind spots, and trust from different points of view. Whether you write the words, doodle images, or draw pictures to get your truth out on paper is up to you. Perhaps you want to record your answers using an app on your phone or computer and then play the answers back to yourself. There are a number of ways for you to answer these questions. Use the method which works best for you.

Checklist A

- ☐ Meetings start late
- ☐ Deadlines are being pushed back due to uncompleted work
- ☐ Don't trust team members to complete tasks
- ☐ Blame others, circumstances, and processes for failures
- ☐ Don't know where team members are in the project
- ☐ Fail to keep your promises, agreements and commitments
- ☐ Micromanage and resist delegating.
- ☐ Inconsistency between what you say and how you behave
- ☐ Scapegoating others
- ☐ Gossip to others about people on your team
- ☐ Promise something you aren't sure you can do
- ☐ Hope problems will go away if ignored
- ☐ Refuse to be held accountable by your colleagues.
- ☐ Use personal misfortune to gain favours at work
- ☐ Cheat - taxes, diet, marriage, cards, etc
- ☐ Don't ask colleagues for help
- ☐ Scared of employee reviews
- ☐ Refuse to follow through on decisions
- ☐ Secret back-door negotiations to create alliances
- ☐ Refuse to apologize

Checklist B

- [ ] You are always on time or 10 min early
- [ ] Loyal to your spouse, friends, and team members
- [ ] Are striving to be a better version of yourself
- [ ] Understands failures are part of the process not a fault
- [ ] Is a resource of information for others to go to
- [ ] Can count on them to get the job done
- [ ] Enables teammates to do their job
- [ ] What you see is what you get
- [ ] Takes responsibility for actions
- [ ] Willing to fix problems
- [ ] Are transparent with intentions
- [ ] Say what you mean and mean what you say
- [ ] Mediates conflict
- [ ] Shares appropriate personal stories
- [ ] Have nothing to hide, welcome the tax audit
- [ ] Asks for help
- [ ] Focused on solutions not problems
- [ ] Apologizes for mistakes
- [ ] Rarely miss a deadline
- [ ] People trust them

If checklist A: you need help. Your team may be engaging in negative conflict behaviour with each other and are not working together to meet your organization's objectives.

If checklist B, you have a team who engages in positive conflict behaviours to work together to move towards your team's objectives.

If checklist A & B are approx. equal, you have a team of mixed conflict behaviours, which is impeding your team's overall success. You will need to work with your team to build healthy conflict discussions.

Go back and make a list of those behaviours from Checklist A, which you will need to be aware of and find solutions to in order to move team members from negative conflict to positive conflict.

Matrix
Accountable

Matrix

Accountability is difficult for some because they don't want to have to answer to anyone if they don't get work done or deliver something that is not good enough. When we are held accountable, we have a light shine on our actions, choices, and excuses. We are vulnerable because someone is going to judge our actions and ask hard questions to ensure we are on target. Leaders need to hold their team members accountable by asking the hard questions. I avoided those hard conversations with my team members. I didn't want to participate in any conflict type conversation. I was scared of what they would say and thought they might get upset with me and leave the company. I didn't trust them to be committed to Matrix and by not holding them accountable, I was not committed to the results I wanted.

My fear of abandonment blindspot drove my avoidance behaviours. This blindspot started with the death of my father and was added to by the deaths of my grandfather and my cousin before I'd become an adult. As each loved one left my world, I became more lost and started getting into trouble. They'd left me to the challenges of the world without their guidance or support and I spiraled out of control. It took almost being killed in an armed robbery and subsequently being arrested for assaulting the robber for me to hold myself accountable for my choices and my future.

Luckily, my brother was there to help me find my future by suggesting I take certain courses to become certified for an IT profession. My life turned around but that fear of abandonment stayed with me and got in the way of my having the hard conversations to keep my staff and myself accountable to our goals.

There is bad conflict and there is good conflict. Do you avoid conflict? Do you use conflict to get your way? Are you angry or scared during conflict? Conflict has a positive outcome when people show up to it with respect for all participants.

Conflict is where we go to define our opinion and voice our wants and needs. It doesn't have to be a battle ground. It can be a place of mutual respect in the pursuit of truth. For this to happen you have to understand your own relationship with conflict and how your behaviour affects others.

Held Accountable

You've promised yourself to eat better and lose weight. You go to the grocery store and buy lots of fruits, vegetables, lean meats, and some diet-based snacks to help relieve some of the cravings you have. You stop by the local gym and sign up for some exercise classes. You are feeling positive about the whole experience and the first week goes pretty good.

Then as time goes on, you find excuses to not go to exercise class because, let's face it, you have a lot of other responsibilities and you are too tired to exercise. Three weeks in, something goes wrong at work and your boss yells at you, so you stop by the store to buy some chocolate and maybe some ice cream. Before you know it, you are no longer on your diet and you've gained whatever little amount you lost back.

Why does this happen? It isn't because you aren't serious enough, it's because you aren't holding yourself accountable or do not have someone holding you accountable. It's natural to not want to be held accountable because it can highlight our failures. No one wants to face their weaknesses or their failures, you are not alone.

169

However, accountability is about ensuring we stay on task, complete the things we start and keep moving forward even when it is too hard. Without accountability we flounder.

What is Accountability?

According to Webster's dictionary, accountability means an obligation or willingness to accept responsibility or to account for one's actions.

Accountability is when you can trust people to deliver on a project or a commitment when they said they would. The second part of accountability is having faith in yourself to deliver on the promises you made so others will trust you. Accountability is what builds trust in our relationships because we are ensuring we take responsibility for our promises. We are respecting others and ensuring they know they can count on us in the future. Accountability is the actions we take when a promise is broken, an excuse is made, or a deadline is casually pushed out. We can choose to not hold someone accountable and ignore the issue, or, we can step up and confront the problem by having hard conversations with them or ourselves. When we do not take responsibility for ensuring our promises are met, we cannot successfully demand others take responsibility for theirs. It starts with us through example and ends with us through communication of expectations. Accountability used to be an issue for me because I lacked trust in others.

I wasn't able to hold people accountable because I never trusted them and if I couldn't trust them, I couldn't have the tough conversation to hold them accountable. Instead, I would say things like, "Can you just get that done for me?" I wouldn't explain that I needed it done by a certain time and ask if they were able to do it. I didn't hold people accountable to the task at hand because I didn't trust they'd stay if I held them to a deadline or a level of excellence. When you are not being accountable to yourself, you do not take responsibility for what you promise to do because you don't trust the process to get it done. You won't hold yourself accountable if you have limiting beliefs about yourself, don't care about your performance, and do not trust yourself to do the job you promised to do.

It's easier to let the deadline pass, to only do the minimum of effort, or to produce at a level of, "Good enough," than it is to have tough conversations with yourself and those who rely on you. If you don't do what you said you were going to do, it affects other people who will either have to initiate a difficult conversation with you or do the work themselves.

Limiting beliefs like "I'm not good enough" will always come into play when we fail to be accountable because if I'm not good enough, I don't trust the process. If I don't trust the process, how am I going to hold myself accountable? It's a cycle, which starts when we agree to do something we don't think we can do because we feel pressured or it's part of our job and we are scared others will find out we can't do it. It is the same reason why we don't start the task and hope it goes away because we believe we can't figure it out, proving we don't belong in the role, in the relationship, or with the company. We hope it will go away because our manager won't want to have the hard conversation and will eventually give the task to someone else to complete.

There is also the other side of the coin where we want to try lots of different things. We start projects but then they get hard, boring, or something more interesting comes along and we're off on another project. People who suffer from shiny object syndrome won't hold themselves accountable because they are on to the next shiny thing, which is a better idea than the last one, or so goes the promise. And of course, nothing ever gets done.

A lot of people, like myself, are a quick start. My Kolbe index says I will start new projects on an ongoing basis because I get bored easily. However, it also says I will finish them. My history shows I'm naturally a great starter but I'm not as good as a finisher. I have worked hard to hold myself accountable and ensure I finish what I start and stay focused. I still stray off the road after a shiny object or two, however, I have a great coach who holds me accountable. He shines the light on those shiny objects to show me that they aren't part of the plan, and they don't fit, as they blind me from my ultimate goal. He helps me to keep myself accountable and to complete the work I set out to do.

Blind spots affect every aspect of your life, how you show up in relationships, and how you react to others. Every single one of your actions causes either a positive or negative impact on others, who then react either positively or negatively towards you. This cycle can cause an issue to escalate out of control or an emotionally charged situation to explode. In a professional environment these reactions can impact a person's future opportunities for advancement and the team's effectiveness to succeed. As a leader, you will need the tools to understand the situation and how to defuse any negative emotional build up.

Avoiding Accountability Behaviour

We behave in certain ways when we aren't held accountable to the people on our teams, which affects our ability to succeed. Leaders who avoid accountability will create ineffective teams because they are creating an apathetic environment of mediocrity. Here are some of the behaviours avoiding accountability created in people.

In Sales:

Every single salesperson hates to be held accountable, and yet, the nature of their job means they have to be accountable all the time. If they are not accountable to themselves, their manager will be accountable to them, which means they will have to sit through tough conversations to explain why they didn't meet their quotas, targets, or promises.

When it comes time to set sales goals some salespeople may set low goals by saying they'll bring in $50 000 in sales this quarter when they have been bringing in $70 000 to $120 000 the last two quarters. This ensures they won't be held accountable if they do not do as well as in the past. Others will come in at $30 000 every quarter and won't push themselves to achieve higher because they don't want to be held accountable for better results. The blind spots they might be experiencing are feelings of not being good enough, avoiding conflict, or a lack of trust in the process or themselves. Lots of salespeople have a problem with being on time and they don't hold themselves accountable to the meeting times they set. If you tell a customer you'll show up at 3:00 but you show up at 3:15 without letting them know you were going to be late, you are not holding yourself accountable and you've broken trust with your client or potential client. They do not worry about being late because they start out running late. It's a way of life to be going full speed from one thing to the next, just to look busy. They are not focusing on what they need to focus on. They are doing something to show they are good enough; they may not be getting the sales but look at how hard they are working, something will close if they just stay busy. In the end, the only result they show is empty promises and unmet goals.

In Leadership:

Leaders who are unable to hold people accountable are trying to hide a limiting belief. Maybe they were pushed too much to achieve and they don't want to make others feel the way they felt when being held accountable. Parents who push their kids are an example of this. "Do homework, read five books, do these extracurricular activities, and you must go to Harvard." It's push, push, push, push. When the child grows up, they go the opposite direction and choose not to push others to achieve or produce, and by doing so, they avoid the accountability conversation.

Then there are the leaders who don't hold themselves accountable. They may go from one idea to the next without ever committing to a process, so they get nowhere. They do a lot of busy work without being accountable to producing results and in the end, they let others down. Since they are always changing their minds about what their team needs to do, they break trust with their team.

Leaders will say, "We're doing something different again and we are going to get this result from it." The team will say, "You said this to me last time and there was no result, I don't believe there will be one this time." The leader basically broke all trust with their team and that's huge because there is no accountability without a strong foundation of trust. So, if a leader breaks that trust, they will need to do all the work to rebuild it, which is harder once trust is broken.

If there is no trust there will be no commitment and accountability becomes, "I need this now. Where is it? I asked for this yesterday."

This opens teams up to fear-based behaviours and lower productivity. This is how important it is to build trust, be committed to the plan, and hold yourself and others accountable to completing their parts. Leaders can become more concerned with their own careers, goals, and desires than what is best for the team or the organization. A leader who is not committed is always looking for the next opportunity for them instead of producing the best results for the task at hand.

In Service:

Customer Service is about delivering what you promised, on time and on budget. However, sometimes the company is unable to deliver on its promise, which is when customer service needs to amend the promise to stay accountable. There are two things a company can do. One, they can choose not to deliver anything and say, "I can't do this because I'm overworked." Second thing they can do is call up the client and say, "I won't be able to get the deliverable sent today. Would you mind if I send it tomorrow?" This is what accountability is about. It is open communication to ensure the customer understands what is happening and ensuring you do your best to deliver what you promised.

Accountability and customer service are about managing expectations to find a compromise when you are unable to deliver on your promise. For example, if I was taking a car into service today because I am planning a trip for tomorrow, the person at the desk doesn't know I'm planning to go away. All the service professional knows is that I need my car serviced. However, I'm holding them accountable because if that car doesn't get done, I can't go on my trip, even though I haven't communicated this to the service professional. If they say it's going to be one o'clock and when I show up at one, the car hasn't even been looked at, there is going to be an accountability problem. Had the service person called me to advise me there was going to be a delay, I could communicate my intention of leaving tomorrow and he would be able to manage the priorities of the shop accordingly. Customer service's job is to manage the accountability of the company.

Accountable Behaviour

When we are held accountable, it shows, and everyone wins because stuff gets done. Leaders who hold their people accountable have boundaries, clear expectations, and drive results. Opportunity flows to accountable teams because they work together to get the job done.

In Sales:

When salespeople are held accountable they hit targets and set new higher ones because they are driven to improve their results. They don't need to be micromanaged or waste time on morning meetings because they get up and start their day knowing what they need to do and are committed to getting it done. These are the high performers who understand what their job is and love to do it.

You can tell if a salesperson is accountable if they show up, they do the work, and they obtain the results they promised they would.

In Leadership:

Leaders who hold themselves accountable are clear on their directives and have set deadlines, which they will meet. They understand what it takes to get the results they are expected to get and keep themselves on task. They are willing to take responsibility when they fail and strive to do better the next day.

Leaders who hold their teams accountable, clearly communicate why they are asking for each deliverable, the expectations, and deadlines. If a team member doesn't meet the expectations, they will have the tough conversation to hold them accountable to the job and expected results.

In Service:

Client service teams who are held accountable understand the customer's needs and the needs of the organization. They are able to solve problems and ensure satisfaction because they know what they can do to solve the problem in front of them. They know why they are there and know where to go for help and support to solve a problem. Every day they are completing tasks the right way to move the organization towards the desired result.

When people are accountable for their own decisions, work, and results, the effectiveness of an organization can greatly increase Holding yourself accountable is very difficult. First, you need to have a group of mentors and peers whom you trust, and they trust you. Second, have a set routine. Share your routine with your peers because once you share your routine, your outcomes, your objectives, and your results, you are accountable to getting the work done. Once you say it out loud, that's a form of accountability. Third, work with a mentor to understand why you want to achieve your goals. A mentor will help you understand what the end results are going to look like and will outline the steps you need to take to get there.

If you have the right peer group, whom you trust, you won't want to let them down, as they will hold you accountable to your commitments. This works because they only have your best interest in-mind and you reciprocate by holding them accountable and having their best interests in-mind. It is about supporting each other, inspiring each other, helping each other, and holding each other accountable.

If you are a manager and want to hold your team accountable, you have their best interest in-mind because it's not about you. When you say, "I need you to deliver that ticket by close tomorrow," it isn't about them, it's about you and what you want. They have to understand how doing the work is going to benefit them in the long run. When you see the work as teaching them to improve themselves, and a way to achieve their goals, then they will be more open to being held accountable by you.

Why do we avoid things we need to do?

It's too hard to do the real stuff. It takes commitment and time and it's not fun. My extrovert personality always requires conversations, so I would rather have a conversation than do the grunt work. Reading a page of a manual is way too much work for me, but getting on a zoom call with somebody, that's easy. However, I started asking myself after I finished the zoom calls, why did I make the call? What was the purpose? I could have read five pages in that amount of time. The answer is simple, we do the fun stuff.

A part of accountability is staying on track and staying the course. Most business owners have a plan outlining the goals of the company and how they will meet those goals. They follow the plan until life happens and they get off track and stop doing the daily tasks which will help them achieve their goals.

Sometimes, the problem is they stop holding themselves accountable for the small daily tasks, which they do not enjoy doing. However, sometimes there is a change in their industry, the economy, or government legislation. Suddenly, they feel a need to pivot, like most businesses did during the Covid-19 shut down.

When the Pandemic shut the economy down, businesses had to pivot and make a new plan to provide their clients and customers with what they did before. Pivoting during these times makes sense and is not a distraction due to a lack of commitment or accountability. In this case pivoting and change is necessary to survival. That is, unless a leader is suddenly doing something so far removed from their core business their customers are no longer receiving what they need. Pivoting is about course correction based on outside circumstances. Following the next shiny trend and abandoning past plans is not being accountable or committed to your success.

Accountability comes when people take responsibility for their work and the promises the organization makes. The whole organization must respect those who hold themselves accountable and take responsibility for their mistakes by fixing them and en- suring the expected results are met. By focusing on individual and team accountability instead of allowing blame and avoidance, orga- nizations are able to have a results based focus.

Ask Yourself in Hindsight

Deep Dive

In this part of the book you are given lots of space to write, doodle, and draw, to understand your level of trust and those who trust you. This isn't a test. I will never see your answers, neither will anyone else if you don't want them to. This exercise and all the other exercises in this book are meant only for you. This is your truth. If you want to discover your truth, then you must be 100% honest with yourself.

The questions are meant to get your mind thinking about behaviour, blind spots, and trust from different points of view. Whether you write the words, doodle images, or draw pictures to get your truth out on paper is up to you. Perhaps you want to record your answers using an app on your phone or computer and then play the answers back to yourself. There are a number of ways for you to answer these questions, use the method which works best for you.

Checklist A

- [ ] Are told how to do each task
- [ ] Don't feel heard by leadership
- [ ] Leadership demands accountability
- [ ] Unsure which results are expected
- [ ] Team members lie about their progress
- [ ] Managers are secretive and passive in their direction
- [ ] Suspect they will be taken advantage of
- [ ] Constantly question the motives of leadership
- [ ] Fear others will steal the credit for their work
- [ ] Aren't sure about the organization's vision
- [ ] Not sure about what the organization's KPIs
- [ ] Are often confused and need to ask constant questions
- [ ] Don't know how things work
- [ ] There is little training or resources to do the job
- [ ] Not sure why they were hired and if they are needed
- [ ] Leadership doesn't listen or allow feedback
- [ ] Can't affect change in the organization
- [ ] Don't take on challenges
- [ ] Not innovative
- [ ] Spread pessimism

Checklist B

- [ ] Clear guidelines and tasks every day
- [ ] Have a voice and feel their ideas are valued by leadership
- [ ] Do the job without having to be asked
- [ ] Know what the end result needs to look like
- [ ] Meets deadlines and KPIs consistently
- [ ] Can count on them to get the job done
- [ ] Honest about where they are in the process
- [ ] Deliver results which meet or exceed expectations
- [ ] Takes responsibility for actions
- [ ] Know where the person stands on an issue
- [ ] Makes his opinions known and supports teammates
- [ ] Share ideas and engages with the team to work together
- [ ] Understands where to go for help and support
- [ ] Will take responsibility for mistakes
- [ ] Feel they have the power to make change
- [ ] Asks for help
- [ ] Leadership listens and is open to honest feedback
- [ ] Looks to expand skill set and take on new challenges
- [ ] Have clear personal goals and team goals
- [ ] Collaborates with others team members

Which checklist has more checkmarks? A or B?

If checklist A, you need help, your team may be engaging in negative conflict behaviour with each other and are not working together to meet your organization's objectives.

If checklist B, you have a team who engages in positive conflict behaviours to work together to move towards your team's objectives.

If checklist A & B are approx equal, you have a team of mixed conflict behaviours, which is impeding your team's overall success. You will need to work with your build healthy conflict discussions.

Go back and make a list of those behaviours from Checklist A, which you will need to be aware of and find solutions to move team members from negative conflict to positive conflict.

Ask yourself

Following are a number of questions with space for you to place your answers to help you redefine your team and yourself to be more trusting and supportive of each other.

Do you make promises but conveniently leave out when something is going to happen?

Do you avoid performance reviews?

Is your team missing deadlines for no reason?

How does avoiding accountability affect your team?

Do you hear a lot of excuses?

Do your leaders bring work to your team because they know you will get it done?

When your team missed a major deadline, what was the reason and how could you have motivated them?

Why is accountability easy or difficult for you?

How do you want your team to perform?

When someone holds you accountable for a task you didn't do, how do you feel? Describe what happens.

Do you avoid the conversation?

Do you give a lot of excuses?

Do you blame others?

Do you come with a plan to complete the project?

Make a list of tasks you need to do to accomplish your goals.

Put a date to be completed beside each of these items and give it to someone you trust to hold you accountable and set a meeting time to go over what you were able to accomplish and what you didn't get done.

Matrix Results
Matrix

	Known to Self	Not Known to Self
Known to Others	Open	Blind Spot
Not Known to Others	Hidden	Unknown

Matrix

As I took personal development courses, I learned more about myself, my limiting beliefs and what I knew I didn't know. The first step to coming to these realizations was understanding that I needed self-awareness. I needed to know myself and had to be present with myself. To achieve this, I learned a technique called the "Johari window."

Imagine a quadrant with four windows in it. The top left corner is called the "Arena" or "Open Area." This quadrant represents what is known by the person about themselves and is also known by others. The top right corner represents what is unknown by the person about themselves, but which others know; this is called the "blind spot area." The bottom left corner, called the hidden area, is what the person knows about themselves that others do not know. Lastly, the bottom right corner is called the unknown area. This represents what is unknown by the person about themselves and is also unknown by others.

Ideally, we want to grow in all quadrants. The blind spot quadrant is the hardest, because often, it's scary to face the truth.

Do we really want to hear about what people have to say about us, especially since we don't believe it ourselves? If we truly want peace and self-awareness, we need to work on our shortcomings and have a greater impact on the people around us.

This is where the role of personal development comes in, whether through masterminds, seminars, or networking events.

When my wife Sam picked me up at the airport after one transformative seminar, I was telling her about the trip and what I'd learned.

"Oh and the stutter is gone!" I said. On the plane I'd struck up a conversation with the lady beside me and noticed I was talking without the stutter. This was life changing for me and the stepping stone for my new career as a speaker.

To improve my speaking skills, I signed up to a course provided by Heroic Public Speaking out of New Jersey. It was an incredible experience to learn acting techniques to improve upon my keynote speeches. During the course I learned more about how I showed up in a room and was encouraged to ask others I trusted how they perceived me based on my behaviours. This exercise taught me about cognitive blind spots and how they affect our ability to show up authentically. These automatic behaviours which are rooted in past experiences get in the way of our success because there is a disconnect between who we think we are and how we are perceived to be.

As my career path began to go in a new direction, I started looking for the right person to purchase Matrix IT. It was important to me that the new IT company was focused on customer relationships and not transactions. My team worked hard to shift our focus back onto the relationship from a transaction based approach and I wanted to do the best I could for my clients and staff. After a few false starts, I sold accounts to IT professionals who would take care of my clients.

I learned a lot of lessons about business from Matrix. I was able to learn from the mistakes I'd made, and the successes that resulted from correcting those mistakes, to become more results focused. When the team started to understand the result we wanted for Matrix and our clients, we were able to grow the company into a successful enterprise.

Results Focused

Results Focused

"What do you really believe makes a difference in the company? For me it's really clear. It's about customers and employees. Everything else follows. If you take care of your customers and you have motivated employees, everything else follows."
– Anne M. Mulcahy

Results based organizations and leaders focus on the result, solving the problem of the customer. They are able to do this because they have built trusting relationships with the customer and the employees. They are willing to engage in healthy conflict to debate issues and find the best solutions for the organization, team, and customer. Leadership is committed to the plan, the vision, and mission of the organization to deliver results and ensure the customer receives what they purchased. They can do this by being accountable to themselves and by holding their teams accountable to ensure the necessary tasks get done to deliver the promised result within the time frame they committed to.

What does a results-based organization look like?

Leaders who are results driven will focus on the team's goals to meet the overall goals of the organization. Teams who are results driven achieve more because they are not focused only on their individual goals and they work together to deliver the expected results. This collaborative team attitude is set by the leadership. Leaders who are more concerned with their own personal results and goals instead of the team's or the organization's, will create a competitive environment where team members feel they need to put their goals before the organization's in order to get ahead.

Results based organizations provide the customer with what they really need, even if they don't understand that need. For example, I go into a car dealership to buy a car, but that's not what I am after. I'm really after a method of transportation which will safely take my family where they need to go. I want to feel safe, cared for, and I want to fulfill my vanity by purchasing a nice vehicle. The salesperson needs to discover what I need before solving my problem by showing me the features and benefits of each vehicle. To be able to fulfill my need, the salesperson must take the time to build trust, so I will open up about what I really am there for. He or she has to be committed to helping me solve my problem and ensuring I get what I am there for. Then they have to hold themselves and others accountable to ensure the vehicle I purchased is delivered to me when promised. If organizations want results, they need to be able to build trusting relationships, commit to the task, and be accountable to get the job done.

If the car salesman is only interested in the transaction and getting cars out the door, he will become frustrated because the process will fall apart either during the sale, after the sale, or when the vehicle is delivered to the customer. This is because people don't always know what they want, they only know they have a problem and are looking for a solution.

If you think about a service advisor who is checking in a customer, and their expected result is to up-sell every single thing possible, then the customer's trust is already broken. They came in for an oil change and are now being told they need to spend a lot of money on other things they didn't know were a problem. They aren't sure these things are necessary because they haven't experienced any issues while driving the vehicle. If the expected result of the service advisor is to take care of the customer to ensure satisfaction, then they will behave differently with the customer. They will start with the customer's experience with the vehicle and determine their expectations from this visit. They will build trust with the customer by being honest and upfront, so when a problem is detected, there is a level of trust in what the service advisor is saying. This happens when the whole organization behaves with integrity, is committed to the customer's satisfaction, and is accountable to delivering on promises.

Results can be measured by Key Performance Indicators, tasks, goals, and balance sheets. However, leaders who lead from the trenches instead of from behind spread sheets have a different measurement of results. They measure the softer targets; things like customer satisfaction, employee retention, training, and growth of the organization in relation to its vision and mission. They understand the process and trust it to provide the financial goals of the organization.

Building a results-based organization starts at the bottom of an organization. Results based leaders will ask employees questions, listen to their answers, reward their initiative, and focus on the main result the organization produces, or the solution it provides the customer. These leaders are clear about the result they want and know how everyone in the organization will contribute to that result. They inspire and help employees by ensuring they have the tools to meet clear expectations. They hire the right people because they understand exactly what the organization needs and all decisions are based on achieving the focused result. It takes effort and buy-in from the whole organization. This ultimately results in decisions being easier to make because they are based on clear defined expected results. Leaders who engage in building these types of organizations are servant leaders whose main focus is to serve others and help them achieve results. Do you want to build a results oriented organization?

Ask Yourself
Forward Thinking

This section is about defining what result you want and how you will achieve it. You will be able to come back to these pages to discover if you are on course or have gone off course. By understanding what you want, you will be able to move towards it.

When the Lulu Lemon manager came to Matrix IT to show us how to see the result we wanted, it helped us as a team to understand each other and to put together a plan which was focused on a common result.

Visualize what result you want and describe what you see in writing by answering these questions in the description. It is important to add every detail and how you feel about it.

Who is with you?

_____

_____

_____

_____

_____

What are you doing?

_____

_____

_____

_____

_____

Where are you? When is this?

Why this result?

How do you feel?

N

W

E

S

Now that you know what result you want, you need to break it down so you know how you will achieve it.

Make a list of all the tasks you will need to complete to make this a reality. For those tasks which will need to be repeated consistently, like social media posts, blogs, landing a client, put an M for monthly, W for weekly, D for daily beside them. For those tasks you need only do once, like take a course, write a book, buy supplies, put a dead-line date beside them.

Now that you know what tasks you need to do to achieve the result and when they need to be done, you need to be held accountable to your commitment.

Make a list of the ways you can be held accountable.

Who can you reach out to and ask if they will be a member of your accountability team?

How can your team hold you accountable?

Beside each name, make a note about how they can help you be accountable so you are clear about their commitment when you ask for their help.

What can you provide in return?

_____

_____

_____

_____

_____

Type of person to ask to be a member of your accountability team: Someone you trust

_____

_____

_____

_____

_____

_____

Someone who will commit to the process

Someone who has integrity

Someone who will have the difficult conversations with you

Conclusion

Conclusion

"We all have blind spots – those areas for improvement and growth. As painful as it can be to admit we're doing things we never wanted to do and saying things we never wanted to say, it is this acknowledgement that enables us to take the first step toward change. Be gentle with yourself. Be real with yourself. Take baby steps."
Rhonda Louise Robbins

Our blind spots are a result of our past experiences. They result in behaviours that we don't intend to portray to people which is why we don't understand how people see us. By understanding our blind spots, we understand ourselves better and are able to show up more authentically and less defensive.

If you haven't already, go to LikkyLavji.com and take the Blind Spot assessment to help you discover blind spots to look out for so you can start changing the way you behave.

Once you complete the assessment, you will receive a report about your style and how you may be showing up to those around you. A few days later you will receive reports on all the different blind spot styles so you can understand how those around you might be behaving in contradiction to who they really are.

When we understand why others behave in the way they do, we can start to build better relationships with them. We can work together as a team more effectively and we can help each other achieve the results we want to achieve. By being results focused you will be able to find the success eluding you.

I learned a lot from my time with Matrix IT and have been able to see how my behaviours affected those around me, causing stress and below par results. We did have lots of success and we did plenty right, however it is from our failures we learned how to be better and become better versions of ourselves.

This book was designed to provide you with the tools and insights to help you change your mindset and behaviours by being more self-aware. If you would like help navigating your blind spots and finding new paths to success, go to likkylavji.com and contact me to see how I can help you succeed.

I love helping people discover their true potential and seeing those light bulbs go off when they realize something new or come up with fresh ideas.

No one achieves success alone.
Everyone who was ever successful has had
support and help along the way.

Manufactured by Amazon.ca
Bolton, ON

18956057R00120